SIEGMUND HURWITZ

LILITH – THE FIRST EVE

Siegmund Hurwitz

Lilith – The First Eve

Historical and Psychological Aspects of the Dark Feminine

With a Foreword by
Marie-Louise von Franz

English translation by Gela Jacobson

DAIMON
VERLAG

This English language edition of the original work, *Lilith – die erste Eva, eine Studie über dunkle Aspekte des Weiblichen* by Siegmund Hurwitz, first published in Zurich, Switzerland, in 1980 by Daimon Verlag, was expanded and updated by the author, edited by Robert Hinshaw and translated by Gela Jacobson.

Revised third edition 2009

ISBN 3-85630-732-5

Cover design by Hanspeter Kälin

For my granddaughter Ruth Lena

Contents

Abbreviations

AfO	Archiv für Orientforschung
AO	Archiv Orientální
ARIT	Aramaean Incantation Texts from Nippur
BASOR	Bulletin of the American Schools of Oriental Research
BBES	Bulletin of the Brooklyn Entomological Society
BT	Babylonischer Talmud
CW	Collected Works
GL	Left Ginza
GR	Right Ginza
JAOS	Journal of the American Oriental Society
JE	Jewish Encyclopaedia
JG	Jewish Gnosticism, Merkabah Mysticism and Talmudic Tradition
JKF	Jahrbuch für kleinasiatische Forschung
JNES	Journal of Near Eastern Studies
Jb	Das Johannesbuch der Mandäer
JL	Jüdisches Lexikon
JRAS	Journal of the Royal Asiatic Society
KS	Kirjat Sepher
LVTL	Lexicon in Veteris Testamenti Libros
MAG	Mitteilungen der Altorientalischen Gesellschaft
MAIT	Mandaean Incantation Texts
MGJV	Mitteilungen der Gesellschaft für jüdische Volkskunde
MII	The Mandaeans of Iraq and Iran
ML	Mandaeische Liturgien

OLZ   Orientalistische Literaturzeitung

OR   Orientalia

PWRE   Pauly's Realencyclopädie der classischen
       Altertumswissenschaft. Neubearbeitet und
       herausgegeben von G. Wissowa

RA   Revue d'Assyriologie et d'Archéologie orien-
       tale

RANL   Reconditi della Accademia Nazionale dei
       Lincei

RdA   Rivista di Antropologia

REJ   Revue des Etudes Juives

RHR   Revue de l'Histoire des Religions

RLC   Revue de la Littérature Comparée

RO   W. H. Roschers Ausführliches Lexicon der
       griechischen und römischen Mythologie

SMSR   Studi e materiali di storia di religioni

TZ   Tarbiz

ZA   Zeitschrift für Assyriologie und verwandte
       Gebiete

ZDMG   Zeitschrift der Deutschen Morgenländi-
       schen Gesellschaft

Preface to the English Edition

Many people have suggested to me that I should make my German-language study available to English-speaking readers who have an interest in psychology. I am all the more happy to fulfill this wish, since it gives me the opportunity to make a number of corrections and amplifications.

This present work is based in the main on the first German edition, published in 1980, and its second edition, which appeared in 1983. Since then, several works have been published which deal with the same subject, either in depth or in passing. With just a few exceptions, these were by female psychologists, who clearly find this subject particularly attractive.

I would like to take this opportunity to refer to two factors with which these women writers are confronted. First, not a single one of them has any knowledge of Hebrew – an absolute requirement for an accurate textual interpretation. Scientific research lays a quite special responsibility on the author: it demands a conscientious study of source material in the original. This is also true for so-called interdisciplinary research, though with certain qualifications. In such cases, the occasional use of secondary literature cannot be avoided. But even in this instance, the researcher is obliged to take great care to apply only scientific material that can stand up to stiff criticism. If this requirement is disregarded, the danger arises that what is found in the texts will be just what was projected into them at an earlier stage.

A second factor which seems to me just as important is that the source material under discussion originates without exception from men and is intended for male readers. Judaism has encountered female writers who deal with Judaic research only within the last decade. It must be presumed, therefore, that our material reflects patriarchal-masculine psychology first and foremost; i.e., it is above all about the anima problem of the Jewish male. And it is precisely this point that is almost completely overlooked in the various studies. What corresponds to the inner anima image only applies externally to the real woman in a secondary fashion.

The chapter on "The Alphabet of ben Sira," in particular, has undergone changes, in that another version of the text has been used which has proved to be more accurate as a result of new findings. The corresponding chapter on the power struggle between Adam and Lilith has also been revised, in the light of my studies of recent works on the subject.

My thanks go above all to the publisher, Dr. Robert Hinshaw, who went to great effort to make this publication possible. I also wish to thank the translator, Mrs. Gela Jacobson, who has not only kept as faithfully as possible to the wording in translating this often difficult text into idiomatic English, but has also succeeded in conveying the meaning behind it.

Finally, I would like to thank the Linda Fierz Foundation for its financial assistance, without which this English-language edition would not have been possible.

S.H.

Foreword by Marie-Louise von Franz

Although nowadays the call for interdisciplinary scientific study rings out constantly, it is seldom heeded, simply because it is difficult to show oneself competent in more than one field. In the case of the goddess Lilith, this has created additional difficulties because Lilith has become a theme in the feminist–anti-feminist discussion. The result is that psychological studies, when they consider historical material, often suffer from an inability to portray it seriously. And when historians venture psychological interpretations, these rarely go beyond the trivial. Thus, the contribution of Siegmund Hurwitz strikes me as particularly valuable in that he has done justice to the claims of both disciplines. His psychological interpretation of the dreams and active imaginations of a depressive man probes the depths and his portrayal of Lilith as an ancient mythological illustration of the negative anima – in short, as a corrupter of men – is competent and thorough. By combining the experience of a modern man with this historical material, Siegmund Hurwitz sheds new light on both. That is the point of the Jungian amplification method.

That an unbridled life urge which refuses to be assimilated lies hidden behind depression – that "Saturnian melancholy," as it was called in earlier times – seems to me to be a new and important discovery. Siegmund Hurwitz has not only demonstrated this among much else but has also illuminated the manner in which a man can handle his "inner

Lilith" so as to find his way out of the Saturnian melancholy.

This book presents us with a gift not only in its new discoveries, but also in providing a means of coping with them.

First pictorial representation of Lilith
Terra-cotta relief from Sumer c. 1950 B.C.

Illustration 1:
A carved ivory lady (perhaps a cult woman) at her window;
courtesy of the British Museum.

Illustration 3: Amulet for protection against Lilith, Persia, 18th century.

A Lilith bound in fetters is depicted with outstretched arms, and on her body is written: "Protect this newborn child from all harm." On either side of her are the names of Adam, Eve, the patriarchs and matriarchs, and above are the initial letters of a passage from numbers 6:22-27, and below from Psalms 121. (from Scholem: *Kabbalah,* p. 360)

Illustration 2: Silver amulet from Kurdistan. Translation:
Top outer row: 42-letter name (27 letters)
Lower outer row: 42-letter name (15 letters), in the name of
                              Shaddai, Trigrammaton.
Inner Panel, Line1. Lilith
                      2. Aviti, Abizu
                      3. Amrusu, Hakash, Odem
                      4. Ik, Pudu, Ayil, Matruta
                      5. Avgu, Kish, Shatrugah, Kali.

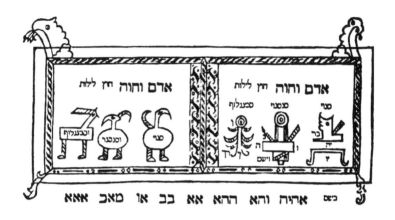

Illustration 4: Protective amulet.

The first illustration of the three angels, *Sanvai, Sansanvai and Semanglof,* sent to bring back Lilith, who had fled from Adam to the shores of the Red Sea, where she was associating with the demons infesting those waters. Lilith refused to return until later so compelled by Elijah the Prophet, whose authority as Sandalphon the Archangel could not be denied. She was forced to accept that the inscription of these three angels' names at childbed would protect against her evil designs. The injunction remains valid to this day and the three names often appear on such amulets designed to protect women at childbirth.

(from T. Schrire: *Hebrew Amulets.* London, 1966, p. 118)

Introduction

This study represents a considerably expanded version of an original short monograph on the Lilith motif in Jewish tradition, which originated as a result of a *dream image* of one of my analysands. The study expanded more and more in the course of time, through consultation with parallel comparative material. From these analytical conversations, it emerged that this figure could not be a form from the world of the dreamer's consciousness but that it exists as a widespread *mythological* motif. However, this led to the question of whether the myth is still living – and, should this be the case, what kind of meaning it has for people today.

In view of the scientific nature of this study, it proved necessary to add a corresponding *scientific apparatus*. This called for a series of studies of complex problems and controversies from the fields of archaeology, Assyriology, epigraphy, Gnosticism, etc. into which this subject had unexpectedly drawn me.

A further difficulty arose from the way in which the question should be formulated. Because a psychologo-religious study was concerned, the available material from mythology, the history of religion, legend, folklore, etc. had to be examined from both the *historical* and the *psychological* standpoint. As a result, a certain danger arose that the reader who was chiefly interested in psychology might make the charge that the study was overweighted with historico-religious material. On the other hand, the religious historian might possibly take a sceptical view of the psychological interpretation of the material or even reject it – and perhaps suspect me of psychologism.

It is difficult if not impossible to stay out of this dilemma completely. All the same, the present study is concerned to do equal justice to both points of view. That is why, in the historico-religious section, all the historical material is examined and an historical commentary is appended in each case. In the psychological section, an attempt is made to demonstrate some psychological aspects of the problem. The present-day importance of the Lilith myth is emphasized by the fact that, in this connection, two spontaneous manifestations from the unconscious of a modern man in which Lilith appears are presented and commented on.

The Lilith motif has received a whole series of literary and pictorial depictions, e.g., – to cite but a few – by Guillaume Apollinaire, Robert Browning, Arthur Collier, Marie Corelli, Gustave Flaubert, Anatole France, John Erskine, Richard Garnett, Victor Hugo, Isolde Kurz, Maurice Magre, John Milton, Dante Gabriel Rossetti, George Bernard Shaw, Wilhelm Martin Leberecht de Wette and Joseph Viktor Widmann.[1] These have not been considered in this survey because I have restricted myself to the mythological and psychological aspects of the problem. In addition, the above-mentioned authors dealt with only one aspect of the Lilith motif in every case, as it were: namely, Lilith in her relations with men, i.e., that side that *C.G. Jung's* psychology usually designates as the *anima*.[2] All the other characteristics that

1. A.M. Killen: *La Légende de Lilith* in ALC, Paris, 1932, Vol. XII, p. 277ff (incomplete)
2. In C.G. Jung's psychology, *anima* denotes the unconscious, feminine part of a man's soul. On the other side of the picture, the woman's *animus* corresponds to the unconscious, masculine part of her personality

Lilith possesses – in legend and folklore, in particular – fail to appear here. In the first place, this must be connected with the fact that, with the exception of *Isolde Kurz,* all the above-mentioned writers are men, on whom this aspect of Lilith naturally makes a special impression.

Apart from a short historical survey in an article by *Gershom Scholem,*[1] a thorough and comprehensive scientific account of this subject has been lacking until now. A psychological interpretation did not exist until this present study appeared. Since then, numerous studies have tried to examine the subject from the woman's point of view, in particular. A series of articles on the subject from the astrological side tried to interpret Lilith, "la lune noire," from this angle. Based on observations made by certain astrologers, *Alfred Fankhauser*[2] had already advanced the assertion that, besides the moon, the earth has another satellite called Lilith. He refers to *A. Jenik*[3] and to a German astrologer named *Walthemath,* who is alleged to have observed and described this satellite of the earth's. In addition, he mentions an astronomer, *M. Gama,* who is supposed to have claimed that Lilith's effects on men are of a highly destructive nature – she causes a certain bestiality and sadism in men whose horoscope is characterized by a dominant Lilith. Fankhauser also refers to a little-known "occult teaching," according to which Lilith's monsters are those who came into being as a result of the "interbreeding of the primeval sons of the gods with animals from the foreworld, i.e., the earliest stages of animal life."

1. G. Scholem: Art. *Lilith in Kabbalah.* Jerusalem, 1974, p. 356ff
2. A. Fankhauser: *Das wahre Gesicht der Astrologie.* Zurich, 1932, p. 32
3. A. Jenik: *Lilith – der schwarze Mond.* Berlin, 1930, p. 154ff

Similar speculations were made by some French astrologers. Thus, *J. Desmoulins* and *R. Ambelain* start out from the allegedly secure hypothesis that Lilith is the second satellite of the earth. Referring to a certain "Docteur Wynn Westcott, particulièrement versé en Kabbale" and also to a writer with the mysterious name of "Sépharial," they assert that Lilith "favorisera le libertinage, les contes gaillards, les conversations perverses" as well as "un certain amoralisme."[1] Other astrologers such as *J. de Gravelaine* and *J. Aimé* at least acknowledge that "L'étude de la Lune Noire se trouvant encore à un stade de recherche, il est prématuré d'affirmer des rapports précis entre les diverses déesses de la mythologie grecque."[2]

I do not wish to enter here into the controversial question of the scientific nature of modern astrology. It seems to be reasonably certain that astrology is not simply a question of an antiquated superstition. As I have been assured by reliable astronomical sources, in the meantime, the existence of a second satellite of the earth can be ruled out with absolute certainty. In this case, the astrologers' speculations clearly represent projections of their spiritual activities into cosmic space, just as, in their day, the alchemists projected their unconscious spiritual contents into the darkness of matter which was unknown to them. Therefore, neither the opinions of the above-mentioned astrologers nor those of the alchemists have any scientific worth. Nevertheless, they do present interesting testimony of the spiritual processes of their authors.[3]

1. J. Desmoulins & R. Ambelain: *Elements d'Astrologie scientifique. Lilith le second satellite de la terre.* Paris, n.d., p. 6
2. J. de Gravelaine & J. Aimé: *Lilith dans L'Astrologie.* Paris, 1974, p. 144
3. After reading this present study, a well-known Swiss astrologer examined my horoscope in accordance with the positions and transitions of Lilith. The prognosticated events of the following five years which were based on this study never actually occurred

Certain psychological studies are considerably more serious than the above-mentioned works.

However, the framework of this present study would be exceeded if I were to take a detailed critical look at all these subjects. So I will give only a quick overview of the work that has appeared since the first edition of this book. I cannot avoid going into somewhat greater detail, though, in the case of certain controversial opinions.

Mention must be made of a short article by *Ean Begg*,[1] based on a seminar given in the Analytical Psychology Club, London. The author tries to uncover connections between Lilith and the black mother goddess. There are no new, original ideas; the author bases himself above all on the work of *Sylvia Brinton Perera*[2] and *Raphael Patai*,[3] as well as on my own study.

Two diploma theses have appeared from the C.G. Jung Institute, Küsnacht, which, among other topics, also deal with the figure of Lilith. They both share the same point of departure – namely, the problem of evil or the demonic and man's attitude toward this question. In her chapter on Lilith, *Anne Lewandowski*[4] uses as her primary source the original manuscript of this present study. *Ethel Vogelsang*[5] deals exclusively with the section of the Lilith myth as it is described in the "Midrash of ben Sira." A further dissertation from the Institute of Applied

1. E. Begg: "From Lilith to Lourdes" in *Journal of Analytical Psychology*, London, 1983, p. 80ff
2. S.B. Perera: *Descent to the Goddess: A Way of Initiation for Women.* Toronto, 1981
3. R. Patai: *The Hebrew Goddess.* Forest Hills, 1967
4. A. Lewandowski: *The God-Image, Source of Evil.* Zurich, 1977, p. 54ff
5. E.W. Vogelsang: *To Redeem the Demonic.* Zurich, 1981, p. 8ff

Psychology in Zurich has been submitted by *Christine Lenherr-Baumgartner.*[1]

Barbara Black-Koltuv's[2] attempt to investigate and interpret the Lilith myth strikes me as rather a failure. Analysts of the Jungian school are not infrequently reproached for carelessness in their pulling together of historical, mythological and ethnological material for the purpose of amplification, in that they tend to find things in texts that they themselves had earlier projected into them. This criticism can well be applied to Koltuv's text. Like her predecessors, the writer in question has knowledge of neither Hebrew nor Aramaic. As a result, she is forced to rely exclusively on secondary literature. To the extent that these sources are reliable, there would be no objections to such a procedure.

The main source used by Koltuv is the Zohar, in the fragmentary and controversial translation by *Harry Sperling* and *Maurice Simon.* Due to the author's one-sided anthroposophic viewpoint, *E. Müller's* unusable translation is also employed. The fundamentally older Midrash, "The Alphabet of ben Sira," is presented in an extremely inaccurate translation. A substantial part of the book consists of personal poems, fantasies and so-called "research" by contemporary women, which at best testify to the personal psychology of their authors. In addition, the detailed bibliography does not list any of the works on this subject that had been previously published, giving the impression that this is the very first publication on the subject. All of these objections lead to the conclusion that this study is scientifically irrelevant.

1. C. Lenherr-Baumgartner: *Lilith-Eva.* Zurich, 1986, p. 1ff
2. B. Black-Koltuv: *The Book of Lilith.* York Beach, 1986

The present study intentionally does not address the motif of "Lilith and the Queen of Sheba" because this has already been covered in a monograph by *Scholem*.[1] However, two further writers – *Rolf Beyer*[2] and *W. Daum*[3] – have also dealt with this subject recently. In her contribution to Daum's book, *A. Klein-Franke*[4] presented a large amount of hitherto practically unknown Yemeni material. *Patai's*[5] book, which has already been mentioned, contains a long chapter on Lilith, which takes a quite general look at the problem of the feminine in Judaism. As this work and my study are partly based on the same source material, a certain amount of overlapping – especially in the chapter on Lilith in Jewish mysticism – cannot always be avoided. But both the point of departure and the objective of the two studies are completely different. While *Patai* approaches the Lilith motif exclusively from the historico-religious viewpoint, I am less concerned with uncovering new historical connections and relations than with uncovering the collective, archetypical background to this myth and bringing out the psychological consequences for modern man which result from this view.

The historical section of this study is based mainly on the results of *Scholem's* modern, historico-religious investigations, while the psychological section is indebted to *Jung's* analytical psychology, especially his teachings on the structural elements of the

---

1. G. Scholem: "Lilith û malkat sheva" in: *Peraqim chadashim me'injeney Ashmedai ve' Lilith*, TZ, Jerusalem, 1947/48, Vol. XIX, p. 165ff
2. R. Beyer: *Die Königin von Saba. Engel und Dämon. Der Mythos einer Frau.* Bergisch Gladbach, 1987, p. 27ff
3. W. Daum: *Die Königin von Saba. Kunst, Legende und Archäologie zwischen Morgenland und Abendland.* Zurich & Stuttgart, 1988
4. A. Klein-Franke: "Lilith in der jüdischen Tradition" in 3), p. 105f
5. R. Patai: *loc. cit.*, p. 207ff

psyche, the Archetypes. Accordingly, a certain knowledge of *Jung*'s psychology is a prerequisite, especially in connection with the psychological section of the study, and in particular as regards the interpretation of the two encounters with Lilith.

From time to time, the material from comparative religious history and from parallel myths, legends and folklore which has been consulted in order to interpret the dreams, and especially the Lilith myth, may seem somewhat farfetched. It should be pointed out, though, that the work of *Jung* and his followers furnished the proof that the so-called *amplification* method – in contrast to the *free association* method employed by *Freud* – is particularly suited to illuminating and clarifying dreams which are difficult to interpret so that they become psychologically comprehensible. However, what is valid in the individual sphere, namely for the *dream* of one single individual, is also valid for the collective contents of the unconscious, which are expressed in myths, fairy tales and legends, etc. Just as the dream of an individual can be described as his *individual myth,* so the myth of a whole people can be described to a certain extent as the *dream of this collective.*[1]

This method of amplification elaborated by *Jung* and further developed by his followers,[2] which draws

1. S. Hurwitz: "Die Gestalt des sterbenden Messias" in *Studien aus dem C.G. Jung Institut, Zürich.* Zurich, 1958, Vol. VIII, p. 11f
2. M.-L. von Franz: *The Passion of Perpetua.* Irving, 1980;
   M.-L. von Franz: "The Dream of Descartes" in *Dreams.* Boston, 1991;
   von Franz: *Die Visionen des Niklaus von Flüe.* Zurich, 1980, 1991;
   A. Jaffé: *Bilder und Symbole aus E.T.A. Hofmanns Märchen "Der Goldne Topf"* in C.G. Jung: *Gestalten des Unbewußten.* Zurich, 1950, Einsiedeln, 1990, p. 239ff;
   E. Neumann: *The Great Mother.* Princeton & London, 1955, p. 13ff

on parallel comparative material from general religious history, comparative mythological research, archaeology, prehistory, ethnology and other sciences, is particularly suited to providing an in-depth understanding of Archetypes and the archetypical images in which these *manifest* themselves. Consequently, according to *Jung*, it is chiefly

"... appropriate when dealing with some obscure experience which is so vaguely adumbrated that it must be enlarged and expanded by being set in a psychological context in order to be understood at all."[1]

But certain dangers exist in the amplification method, just as they do in *Freud*'s free association method: one such danger consists in the possibility that, through an infinitely continued amplification or association, the connection with the point of departure could finally be lost. That is why *Erich Neumann*[2] was right to point out that the amplification should always be followed by a kind of *actualization*, by means of which a reference can be made to the point of departure. Similarly, just as cult and ritual provide a re-experiencing of a single, historical situation, so the personal element is brought into contact with the archetypical background through the actualization of the amplification. At the same time, it isn't enough that the material gained through amplification should be understood exclusively on an intellectual level. It should also be experienced emotionally and comprehensively.

My most grateful thanks go to my late friend Prof. *Gershom Scholem,* Jerusalem, for checking and correct-

1. C.G. Jung: *Psychology and Alchemy,* CW. Princeton & London, 1953, Vol. XII, p. 289
2. E. Neumann: "Die mythische Welt und der Einzelne" in *Kulturentwicklung und Religion.* Zurich, 1953, p. 108f

ing the historical section of this study, as well as for numerous pieces of advice, both verbal and written. I would also like to thank Dr. *Marie-Louise von Franz,* Küsnacht, for correcting the manuscript and also for her willingness to write a foreword to this study. My thanks to Prof. *Joseph Naveh,* Jerusalem, for his comments on the Arslan Tash Inscriptions, to Rabbi Dr. *Jacob Teichmann,* Zurich, for his help in translating the passages from the *Zohar,* and to Dr. *Robert Hinshaw* for his editorial work.

Part I

Historico-Religious Section:

The Myth and its History

May the eye not be turned to the outside
lest it simultaneously drive out the images.
Sister Elsbet Stagel of the Töss Monastery
(14th Century)

1) The Dual Aspect of Lilith

Of all the motifs in Jewish mythology, none – other than that of the Messiah – remains so vivid to this day as the myth of Lilith. She occupies a central place among the demonic images of Judaism because she is by far the most distinctive figure among this religion's numerous evil spirits.

Originally, Lilith was an archaic goddess who, on her very first appearance in the historico-religious tradition, presented just one single aspect: that of a terrible mother-goddess. However, this character changed in the course of the development of the myth. By the time of the Talmudic-Rabbinic and Graeco-Byzantine traditions at the latest, Lilith had acquired a strange dual aspect. Depending on whether she is faced with a man or a woman, one or other side of her becomes more apparent. Faced with a man, the aspect of the *divine whore* or, psychologically speaking, that of the seductive anima comes more to the fore. To a woman, however, she will present above all the aspect of the *terrible mother*. As the anima figure, Lilith attempts to seduce not only the first man, Adam, but also all men, even today – because, according to one of Jewish mysticism's ancient traditions, she is immortal. She will meet her death only on the Day of Judgement.[1]

As the terrible, devouring mother, she tries to harm pregnant women and to steal their newborn children. She is always poised to kill the child so that

1. I Zohar 55a

she can drink its blood and suck the marrow from its bones. This aspect of Lilith is already conveyed in early texts, in which she is called "the strangler."

There are definite historico-religious and psychological reasons why the aspect of the divine whore and seductive anima only appeared much later, historically speaking. The feminine always appears first within the development of consciousness in the form of the Great Mother, who is a bipolar, archetypical figure, in that she contains the aspect both of the nurturing, caring mother and of the terrible, devouring mother. The figure of the anima was only detached from the mother figure in a later phase of consciousness.

The figure of Lilith as we encounter her in Jewish literature is, however, by no means restricted exclusively to Jewish mythology. She occurs among both Semitic and non-Semitic peoples – among the Babylonians, Assyrians, Jews and Arabs on the one hand and among the Sumerians and Hittites on the other. But only in Jewish mythology has the Lilith myth existed for more than two and a half thousand years and has even managed to develop still further. Indeed, its radiations can be traced into the most immediate present: even today, for apotropaic reasons, Orthodox Jewish families, especially in the East and South, hang various amulets in the maternity room or round the necks of the mother and her newborn child to protect them from the dangerous machinations of this ill-omened, demonic figure.

The two sides of Lilith had already been personified in Babylonian literature, in the two goddesses Lamashtû and Ishtar, out of which the figure of Lilith crystallized. For this reason, I have designated them as the *Lamashtû aspect* and the *Ishtar aspect*.

The Babylonian goddess Lilitû later underwent several strange transformations within the Jewish tradition. First, she lost her original divine character and became a colorless, nocturnal desert ghost.

To attain a deeper understanding of Lilith's transformations, it is necessary to make a short digression into Jewish, and from there back still further into Babylonian teachings on demons. Starting from this point, it is possible to illuminate the two opposing aspects of Lilith.

In Jewish literature, Lilith is one of the numerous demons who are mentioned in the Bible, the Talmud and Rabbinic tradition. But even outside this canonical literature, in apocryphal and pseudepigraphic works, in the Aramaic magic texts of Nippur, in Gnostic and Mandaean literature, as well as later in Jewish Mysticism and Jewish popular belief, Lilith occupies a considerable space.

Jewish demons occur under quite different names. One moment they are described as spirits (*Ruchot*), the next as pests (*Masiqim*) and the next as destroyers (*Chabalim*). They can be grouped under the collective name *Shedim,* sing. Shed, Aramaic Shida, i.e., demons. Shedim are either benevolent and helpful, or – more frequently – dangerous troublemakers. On the whole, the demons who meet humans and have dealings with them are male, but now and then there are female ones. From time to time, too, there are goblins or poltergeists – generally harmless and benevolent, though in the habit of teasing humans.

The Hebrew word *Shed* can almost certainly be traced back to the Akkadian word Shedû, which for its part corresponds to the Sumerian word Aladû. In Babylonia, the Shedû was originally a predominantly chthonic deity who was worshipped as a bull with a

bearded human head. The ideograms for bull and
Shedû are identical. At the same time, however, they
are also the same as that for Nergal, the Babylonian
rule of the underworld and the kingdom of the dead,
so that it may be assumed that the Shedû also had
some connection with the souls of the dead.[1]

Since the Shedû is always represented as a winged
bull, it is to be presumed that, as well as his chthonic
aspect, he possessed a spiritual aspect. Facing the
male Shedû is the female Lamassû or Lama, called
Kal in Sumerian and whom the Sumerians portrayed
as a winged cow. In contrast to the rather negative or
ambivalent Shedû, Lamassû is always a kindly and
helpful being. Shedû and Lamassû were erected at
the gate of the palace of King *Assurnazirpal,* and on
his accession to the throne, King *Assarhaddon* prided
himself on having set up Shedû and Lamassû to the
right and left of the palace entrance as guardians of
the royal house and tutelary gods of the Assyrian
people. The Sumerian Lamassû was later included in
the Babylonian pantheon, though in so doing she –
like Shedû – underwent certain transformations, because she was changed into a demon and worshipped as the great and terrifying mother-goddess
Lamashtû, who has lost almost all her positive features.

a) The Lamashtû Aspect

Lamashtû is one of the two original images that
left their mark on the figure of Lilith. She has many
features in common with Lilith. Both watch the preg-

1. S.H. Langdon: "Semitic Mythology" in *The Mythology of all Races.*
   Boston, 1931, Vol. V, p. 358ff

nant woman vigilantly – especially when she is in labor. They try not only to harm her personally, but also to steal her newborn child from her and to kill it. On amulets, both goddesses were named together and enjoined to leave mother and child alone.

A birth scene is depicted in an impression of a Babylonian cylinder seal from the Ashmolean Museum in Oxford, published by *Stephen H. Langdon*[1] and which shortly after was also described by *Bruno Meissner.*[2] According to an interpretation given by *C. Frank,*[3] in this scene, a woman in labor is being attacked by demons led by Lamashtû. However, this interpretation is disputed by *Meissner.*

A few authors have already pointed to a close connection between Lamashtû and Lilith. According to *F. Perles,* it even appears that:

"... in the Jewish consciousness above all, Lamashtû and Lilith are almost identical."[4]

However, this could hardly be the case, since Lilith – along with her Lamashtû aspect – also has other characteristics that Lamashtû lacks completely. On the other hand, it is true that, in the Lilith myth, the Lamashtû aspect is historically older. For this reason, we ought to consider this Babylonian goddess somewhat more closely.

1. S.H. Langdon: "Babylonian and Hebrew Demonology with reference to the supposed borrowing of Persian Dualism in Judaism and Christianity" in IRAS, London, 1934, p. 50
2. B. Meissner: "Neue Siegelcylinder mit Krankheitsbeschwörungen" in AfO, Berlin, 1935/36, Vol. X, p. 160ff
3. C. Frank: "Lamastû, Pazuzû und andere Dämonen. Ein Beitrag zur babylonisch-assyrischen Dämonologie" in MAG, Leipzig, 1941, Vol. XIV, No. 2, p. 5, note 1
4. F. Perles: "Noch einmal Labartû im Alten Testament" in OLZ, Leipzig, 1915, Vol. XVIII, p. 179f

Unlike other frequently rather hazily portrayed Near Eastern goddesses, the personality of the goddess Lamashtû is defined with absolute clarity. The best sources for an understanding of this figure are the so-called Labartû texts[1] published by *D.W. Myhrman.* The texts have been corrected and expanded in certain respects over the last few decades.

In these sources, Lamashtû is always invoked as a goddess. Her father is the Babylonian god of heaven, Anû, and thus she is, generally called simply "daughter of Anû." She is the "chosen confidante" of Irnina, a goddess who is related to the Sumerian Inanna and the Babylonian Ishtar.

The Labartû texts say:[2]

"Her abode is on the mountains, or in the reedbeds. Dreadful is her appearance. Her head and her face are those of a fearsome lion, white as clay is her countenance, she has the form of an ass, from her lips pours spittle, she roars like a lion, she howls like a jackal. A whore is she. Fearsome and savage is her nature. Raging, furious, fearsome, terrifying, violent, rapacious, rampaging, evil, malicious, she overthrows and destroys all that she approaches. Terrible are her deeds. Wherever she comes, wherever she appears, she brings evil and destruction. Men, beasts, trees, rivers, roads, buildings, she brings harm to them all. A flesh-eating, bloodsucking monster is she."

In other texts, it says that she watches the pregnant woman most vigilantly and tries to snatch the new-

1. The older version La-bar-tû has generally been abandoned by modern Assyriology
2. D.W. Myhrman: "Die Labartû-Texte. Babylonische Beschwörungsformeln nebst Zauberverfahren gegen die Dämonin Labartu" in ZA, Strasbourg, 1902, Vol. XVI, p. 148ff (This text is a compilation of four different passages)

born child from her. Some time before the birth, she appears in the maternity room so as to tear the child from the mother's body. Then she begins to torment the child "now with heat and fire, then with fever and shivering."[1]

Images from a magic conception of the world are the basis of the Babylonian magic and incantation texts against Lamashtû, of which a large number have been preserved. In magic, two elements are almost always combined: on the one hand, the sorcerer-priest – who functions as an exorcist – uses incantations to invoke and conjure the goddess; on the other, certain ritualistic magic practices are involved. That is why, in Babylonia, there was a distinction between shiptû and epeshû, and similarly, in the Greek magic papyri, between *logos* and *pragma.*

The *magic practices* consist mostly in an analogous magic carried out according to precise instructions. Various prescriptions for this are given in the Labartû texts. One, for example, advises making a clay figure of the goddess. Twelve loaves and other foods should then be placed before this figure as sacrificial offerings. The figure of a black dog should be placed before the clay figure. After three days, during which the goddess will leave the body of the person she has bewitched and enter the clay figure, this last should be smashed with a sword and the pieces buried in a corner of the city wall, but not before the whole area has been consecrated with flour water.[2] The provision of a pair of sandals to carry the goddess across the river or the sea is also part of the magic practices, whose aim is to drive away Lamashtû or render her

1. D.W. Myhrman: *loc. cit.*, p. 181
2. D.W. Myhrman: *loc. cit.*, p. 161 & 195

harmless.[1] Other prescriptions recommend the preparation of a ship by the priest, in which a picture of Lamashtû, together with pictures of black and white dogs – animals sacred to Lamashtû – should be placed in the hope that the river will carry the ship, and the goddess, away forever.[2] Other magic practices consist in the making of amulets. These are composed of different-colored ribbons and bands wrapped around precious stones. They were tied round the newborn child's neck, wrists and ankles and were intended to protect it.

Quite specific texts, which the priest recited in an order established by tradition, belong to the *invocations and incantations.*

In the Babylonian magic and amulet texts, Lamashtû is seldom mentioned by herself. Mostly, she appears with a group of other related gods or demons. In an incantation text against the so-called *Uttuke group,* it says:[3]

"He, upon whom the evil Uttukû threw himself,
He, whom the evil Alû suffocated in his bed,
He, whom the evil Etimmû overpowered in the night,
He, whom the evil Gallû threatened,
He, whose limbs the evil Ilû tore apart,
He, whom Lamashtû seized and dominated,
He, whom Labashû overpowered,
He, whom Ahhazû held fast, etc."

Among the demons listed, Uttukû and Labashû are known to be fever demons, while Etimmû (alternative spelling: Ekimmû) is some kind of spirit of

1. D.W. Myhrman: *loc. cit.*, p. 149
2. D.W. Myhrman: *loc. cit.*, p. 150
3. H.C. Rawlinson: *Cuneiform Inscriptions of Western Asia.* London, 1861/84, V 51

death. Ahhazû means something like predator, grasper, grabber, while Ilû is the general term for a god or devil. However, it is not easy to tell the individual demons in the group apart; indeed, it is not even possible to say with any degree of certainty what sex they are, which points to the archaic character of this image. Some are neither male nor female, some have changed sex over the course of time. Some seem merely to be different sides of the character of Lamashtû.

What makes these incantation texts particularly interesting are two demons who have a close connection with Lilith, namely Alû and Gallû.

Alû was originally an asexual demon, who later took on female characteristics. Alû is a demon without mouth, lips and ears, half man, half devil. At night, he roams the streets like a masterless dog.[1] Then he creeps into people's bedrooms and terrifies them while they sleep.[2] Alû also appears in Jewish texts under the name *Ailo*. In these, he is one of the secret names of Lilith.[3] However, in other texts, Ailo is described as the daughter of Lilith, who has had a liaison with a man. That demons have sexual relations with men and produce devil children as a result is an idea which occurs in all the Semitic religions. Thus, for example, the pre-Islamic, Arabic, demon literature contains similar liaisons between men and djinn. This idea is also well-known in the Talmud and in Mandaean Gnosticism. Later, too, the notion was taken up in Kabbalistic literature. According to Kab-

1. R.C. Thompson: *The Devils and Evil Spirits in Babylonia*. London, 1903, p. 37
2. G. Contenau: *La Magie chez les Assyriens et les Bayloniens*. Paris, 1947, p. 90
3. J.A. Montgomery: ARIT, Philadelphia, 1913, p. 260

balistic belief, demons don't actually have a body of their own, because the Sabbath intervened before its creation. They need a human body in order to reproduce. As a result, Lilith uses the drops of sperm which are ejaculated during sleep or marital intercourse so as to:

> "...create a body for herself from the sperm which is dropping into the void."[1]

In this connection, *G. Scholem* refers to a Kabbalistic rite – part of which is still practised today – which was carried out at burials in Jerusalem:

> "Ten Jews danced round the dead man and recited a psalm, which was commonly accepted in Jewish tradition as a psalm of protection against demons."[2]

Obviously, what is involved here is an archaic, apotropaic rite, which is directed at those children of the dead man he fathered by a demon. These congregate on the death of their father and demand their paternal inheri-tance. Now and again, they hurl abuse at the dead man's legitimate children or even attempt to attack them physically. This was also the reason why certain 16th-century Kabbalists forbade the sons of the dead man to take part in his funeral.[3]

Another – female – demon of the Uttukû group, who also has a close connection with Lilith, is *Gallû*. Occasionally, this name, like that of Uttukû, is used simply as a general term for all demons, and these are called "evil Uttuke" or "evil Galli":

> "Gallû, the spirit that threatens every house,

1. G. Scholem: "Tradition und Neuschöpfung im Ritus der Kabbalisten" in *Zur Kabbala und ihrer Symbolik*. Zurich, 1960, p. 202
2. G. Scholem: *loc. cit.*, p. 202f
3. G. Scholem: *loc. cit.*, p.205

Brazen Gallûs, seven are they,
They grind the land like flour,
They know no mercy,
Rage at the people,
Eat their flesh,
Let their blood flow like rain,
They never stop drinking blood."[1]

In amulet texts, sometimes it is Lamashtû, sometimes Gallû and sometimes Lilith who is invoked and conjured. Gallû later appeared as Gello, Gylo or Gyllou in Graeco-Byzantine mythology, in which Gyllou has become a child-stealing and child-killing female demon. This figure was also taken up by Jewish mythology, as Gilû. Like Ailo, or Alû, Gilû is also a secret name for Lilith. According to *Bernhard Schmidt*,[2] belief in the Gylloudes is still fully alive in present-day Greece.

The Babylonian magic spells, which were supposed either to drive away the demons who brought illness or other troubles or to render them harmless, had to be recited in a precise order over the individual limbs of the person who had been bewitched, in order to be effective. This is because demons attack only one particular part of the body at any one time – for example, Uttukû the shoulder, Alû the breast, Gallû the hand, Assakû the head and Namtarû the throat.[3] Familiarity with the effects of the demons and, above all, knowledge of their secret names, was supposed to protect people from their machinations.

1. *Cuneiform Texts from Babylonian Tablets in the British Museum.* London, 1896, XVI 14
2. B. Schmidt: *Das Volksleben der Neugriechen und das hellenische Altertum.* Leipzig, 1871, p. 139
3. B. Meissner: *Babylonien und Assyrien.* Heidelberg, 1920, Vol. I, p. 391

All magic spells begin formally with the word *Shiptû*, i.e., incantation.[1] Thereafter, there follow invocations of the various demons or characteristics of a particular demon. Finally comes the demand that they should depart. For example, it says about Lamashtû:[2]

> "Shiptû. Lamashtû, daughter of Anû, is her first incantation.
> The second: Sister of the gods of the streets.
> The third: Sword that splits the head.[3]
> The fourth: She who sets fire to wood.
> The fifth: Goddess whose face is terrifying.
> The sixth: Confidante and chosen one of Irnina.
> The seventh: May you be conjured by the great gods:
> That you may fly away with the bird of the heavens."[4]

In addition to the Labartû texts, a further series of similar magic and incantation texts was published later by *Erich Ebeling*.[5]

Sometimes, the amulets against Lamashtû contain similar incantations and sometimes they carry pictorial representations of the goddess. Some of these amulet texts were published by *Frédéric Thureau-Dangin*. Since then, whole series of similar texts have been discovered in various museums and published.[6] For the most part they are similar to the Shiptû texts

---

1. This corresponds to the word Shifta on Aramaic magic bowls
2. D.W. Myhrman: *loc. cit.*, p. 155, as well as the somewhat different translation by M. Jastrow jun.: *Die Religion Babyloniens und Assyriens.* Giessen, 1915, Vol. I, p. 335
3. Alternative reading: Dagger that splits open the head
4. Alternative reading: With the birds of the heavens
5. E. Ebeling: *Keilinschriften aus Assur religiösen Inhalts.* Leipzig, 1922, p. 175
6. Museums in Berlin, Leiden, Copenhagen, New York etc.

which had already been discovered. Thus, it says of Lamashtû:

> "Dreadful is she, headstrong is she, she is a goddess, terrible is she. She is like a leopard (?), the daughter of Anû. Her feet are those of (the bird) Zu, her hands are dirty, her face is that of a powerful lion. She rises out of the reedbed. Her hair is loose, her breasts are bare. Her hands are caked with flesh and blood. She forces an entry through the window, she slides in like a snake. She enters the house, she leaves the house again."[1]

The figure of Lamashtû or – as she is also known – of *Lammea* later entered Greek mythology as Lamia.[2] According to one version, Lamia was a Phrygian queen; according to another tradition, she was the daughter of a king of the Laistrygons in Libya. She was the beloved of Zeus, to whom she bore a number of children. Hera pursued her out of jealousy and envy and killed all her children except Skylla. From grief, Lamia lost her beauty; and out of jealousy of all mothers who had babies, she tried to seize these children.[3] She has the ability to take out her eyes, so that these remain on watch and can keep a lookout for children while Lamia sleeps.[4] Lamia was depicted as a creature with the body of a snake and the head of a beautiful woman. In antiquity, the name Lamia meant – like Lilith – on the one hand a single being, on the other a multitude of female, child-stealing demons. According to *Schmidt,* even today in Greece there is a belief that:

1. F. Thureau-Dangin: "Rituel et amulettes contre Labartu" in RA, Paris, 1921, Vol. XVIII, p. 161ff
2. W.H. Roscher: RP, Leipzig, 1884/86 cf. lamia
3. PWRE, Stuttgart, 1931, Vol. II cf. lamia
4. K. Kerényi: *The Gods of the Greeks.* London and New York, 1951, p. 38f

"If a youth, especially a well-proportioned one, sings or whistles on the beach at midday or midnight, the Lamia of the sea rises out of the deep and tries to persuade him to become her husband and to come into the water with her, through the promise of a blissful life. If the youth refuses, she kills him."[1]

According to *Karl Kerényi*,[2] the devouring side of Lamia is also expressed in her name, because *laimos* means maw or jaws. However, against this interpretation stands the fact that the origin of the name is most certainly derived from the Sumerian Lammea.

Empousa is also related to Lamia. Like Lamia, she is a ghost related to Hecate, with whom both are identified. *Libanius*[3] reports that Empousa lures men by her charms and then kills and devours them. Empousa, too, lives on in the fairy tales and folklore of modern Greece.[4]

Mormo[5] is a figure related to Lamia and Empousa. It is said of her that she kills and eats even her own children – a characteristic attributed to Lilith as well.

The *Stringes*[6] are other child-stealing beings from Greek mythology. In folk tradition, the Stringes are enchantresses who:

"fly at night in the guise of birds to the cradles of children and suck their blood." [7]

According to another version, they are:

1. B. Schmidt: *loc. cit.*, p. 131
2. K. Kerényi: *loc. cit.*, p. 38f
3. Libanius cited in: RO, cf. Empousa
4. B. Schmidt: *loc. cit.*, p. 141
5. J. Fontenrose: *Python. A Study of Delphic Myth and its Origin.* Berkeley & Los Angeles, 1959, p. 116
6. RO: cf. Stringes
7. B. Schmidt: *loc. cit.*, p. 136

"Women who journey at night through the air and force their way into houses – however securely fastened – and strangle tiny children or devour their liver."[1]

These Stringes live on today as Strigais or Striglais in contemporary Greek popular belief, and also in Neo-Greek folk tales and legends.

The *Striges* of Roman mythology are connected with the Greek Stringes. They, too, are child-stealing, bloodsucking, female demons. They have the body of a bird and the head of a seductive woman. Ovid says of them:

"Greedy birds are they,
They fly around at night.
They seek out children, when their wet-nurse is away.
They carry them off.
They maul their bodies with their claws.
They are said to tear out the entrails of the baby
                                        with their claws.
Their maw is full of the blood that they drink.
Striges is their name."[2]

In a popular legend from the end of the 17th century cited by *Max Grünwald*,[3] written in the Yiddish language,[4] which also found its way into Kabbalistic literature, an angel by the name of *Astaribo* is mentioned. He meets the prophet Elijah. An analogous amulet text from around the same time describes the prophet's meeting with Lilith. Astaribo also tries to strangle small children, to drink their

1. B. Schmidt: *loc. cit.*, p. 136
2. Ovid: Fastae 131ff
3. M. Grünwald: MGJV, Hamburg, 1898, No. 5, p. 48
4. Yiddish is a mixture of Middle High German and Hebrew with East European words

blood and to eat their flesh. *Scholem*[1] has established that the name Astaribo should correctly be read as Astriga or Striga. He is of the belief that the name Astaribo-Astriga-Striga derives originally from Hystera, the demon who spells danger for the mother's womb *(hystera)*. In a marginal note to a 14th-century Oxford manuscript which contains parts of the early-mystical so-called Hechalot literature, there is the following verse:

> "Black Striga, black upon black,
> Blood will she eat, blood will she drink.
> Like an ox will she bellow,
> Like a bear will she growl,
> Like a wolf will she crush people to death."

Demonic figures akin to Lamias and Striges appear in the mythology of almost all peoples. Either they are child-stealing, bloodsucking beings, or they appear as seductive women. There are myths in which both aspects occur simultaneously.

Indeed, this motif of the child-stealing witch and the seductive woman is a universally occurring, i.e., archetypical motif. This can be proved without difficulty, since the image occurs in cultures which are so far apart that any influence through migration can most definitely be ruled out. Thus *W.W. Skeat*[2] has pointed to the image of the *Langsuir,* also known as Langsuyar, in Malaysia, which is supposedly common knowledge in that country. The Langsuir is a female demon, who appears either as a predatory night owl

1. G. Scholem: "Relationship between Gnostic and Jewish Sources" in JG, Philadelphia, 1965, p. 27, note 27, cf. G. Scholem: Buchbesprechung von H.A. Winklers Buch: "Salomo und die Karina" in KS, Jerusalem, 1934/35, Vol. X, p. 72
2. W.W. Skeat: *Malay Magic.* London, 1900, p. 326

or as a seductive woman. In contrast to the magic practices employed by the Babylonians against Lamashtû, in Malaysia it is recommended that the Langsuir should be caught. Then her overlong fingernails should be cut off and her thick hair should be stuffed into a hole in her neck. In this way, the Langsuir will be completely tamed and "will be indistinguishable from a normal woman for many years." This woman stands out because of her dazzling beauty. From time to time, too, she may assume her original form once more and return to the dark forest from which she first came to men. If such a Langsuir woman brings a dead child into the world, then it – like its mother before it – is a demon in the form of a night owl. That is why various magic practices are recommended in order to prevent such a stillbirth.

In this connection, it may be of interest to investigate a linguistic problem, namely the question of how and under what meaning the name Striga has been preserved in various languages. The connection between the motifs of the night owl, the seductive witch and Striga shows up clearly when we compare the various Romance languages with one another.

In *zoology*, owls are commonly classified as Strigiformes. A subdivision consists of owls in the strict sense of the term, or *Strigidae*. To this group belongs the screech owl or *Strix*, known for catching small mammals.[1]

In Italian,[2] the word *strega* means something akin to an evil old woman or witch, who is in league with

---

1. B. Grzimek: *Grzimeks Tierleben.* Zurich, 1969, Vol. VIII, cf. owl
2. F. Palazzi: *Novissimo Dizionario della Lingua Italiana.* Milan, 1974, cf. strega or strige

the devil. In *Old French*,[1] the word is estrie and means
a vampire-like creature. The *Portuguese*[2] parallel, estria, means witch. She corresponds to the Spanish
bruja. In *Rhaeto-Romanic*[3] – and, in fact, in both the
Ladin and Surselvan dialects – the word is stria. But
in all languages, so to speak, the word means a witch
on the one hand and a predatory night owl on the
other. This appears most clearly in Italian, where the
strige are "una famiglia di uccelli notturni" and in
Romanian,[4] where striga means a night owl. But in
non-Romanic languages, too, the striga is well-
known. In the *Balkans,* her name is *strygoi*.[5] Perhaps
the Swiss German name Sträggele, which is used in
popular belief in the Middle Reuss district, i.e., the
cantons of Lucerne and Aargau, is also connected
with the term striga. The Sträggele, who generally
appears in the company of a male companion, the
Thürst, is a witch who carries off disobedient children and lazy girls.[6]

In the following section, we will firstly consider the
strange name of Lilith. The Hebrew word Lilith –
Lilita in Aramaic – makes its first appearance in a
fragment of a Sumerian version of the Gilgamesh
epic, which was translated, annotated and published

1. A. Tobler & E. Lomatzsch: *Altfranzösisches Wörterbuch.* Wiesbaden, 1952, cf. estrie
2. J.P. Machado: *Dicionario Etimologico de la Lingua Portugues.* Lis-
   bon, 1952, cf. estria
3. R.R. Bezzola & R.O. Tönjachen: *Dicziunari tudais-ch-rumantsch
   ladin.* Samedan, 1944, cf. witch; R. Vieli & A. Decurtins: *Vocabu-
   lari Romontsch-Sursilvan-Tudesg.* Chur, 1962, cf. stria
4. H. Tiktin: *Rumänisch-deutsches Wörterbuch.* Bucharest, 1912, cf.
   striga
5. T.H. Gaster: *Myth, Legend and Custom in the Old Testament.* New
   York & Evanston, 1969, p. 579
6. Schweiz. Idiotikon: *Wörterbuch der schweizerischen Sprache.* Frauen-
   feld, 1952, cf. Stragg-Strugg

by *Samuel N. Kramer*. The text is based on copies which were prepared from an original draft sometime during the Isin Larsa period (c. 1950-1700 B.C.). The original itself must be appreciably older, and it is believed today to date from the 40-th century B.C. The passage relating to Lilith reads as follows:

> "After heaven and earth had been separated and mankind had been created, after Anû, Enlil and Ereskigal had taken possession of heaven, earth and the underworld; after Enki had set sail for the underworld and the sea ebbed and flowed in honor of its lord; on this day, a huluppu tree (probably a linden tree), which had been planted on the bank of the Euphrates and nourished by its waters, was uprooted by the south wind and carried away by the Euphrates. A goddess, who was wandering along the banks seized the swaying tree and – at the behest of Anû and Enlil – brought it to Inanna's garden in Uruk. Inanna tended the tree carefully and lovingly; she hoped to have a throne and a bed made for herself from its wood. After ten years, the tree had matured. But in the meantime, she found to her dismay that her hopes could not be fulfilled. Because during that time, a dragon had built its nest at the foot of the tree, the Zu-bird was raising its young in the crown, and the demon Lilith had built her house in the middle. But Gilgamesh, who had heard of Inanna's plight, came to her rescue. He took his heavy shield, killed the dragon with his gigantic bronze axe, which weighed seven talents and seven minas. Then the Zu-bird flew into the mountains with its young, while Lilith, petrified with fear, tore down her house and fled into the wilderness."[1]

1. S.N. Kramer: "Gilgamesh and the Huluppu-Tree. A Reconstructed Sumerian Text" in *Assyriological Studies of the Oriental Institute of the University of Chicago.* Chicago, 1938, p. 1f

The name used for Lilith here is *Ki-sikil-lil-la-ke*,[1] i.e., the maiden Lilith. It goes on to say of her in the text that she is a "maiden who screeches constantly" and a "gladdener of all hearts."

The name of her male companion, the god or demon *Lila,* is also known from this period. *Thorkild H. Jacobsen*[2] has pointed out in his work on the names of Sumerian kings, that the father of the hero Gilgamesh was called Lilû (= Lila) or was a Lilû demon. The translation does not indicate clearly whether Lilû was used as the hero's proper name or as a description of his character.[3]

In other Sumerian texts, a further female being – *Ki-sikil-ud-da-kar-ra*[4] – is mentioned alongside *Ki-sikil-lil-la-ke.*

The meaning of the word Lila or Lilû is disputed. If it is derived from the Sumerian, which appears to be correct, then Lila means a kind of storm or wind god. If, on the other hand, one opts for an Akkadian, i.e., Semitic origin, as *Reginald C. Thompson*[5] suggests, then either Lalu, i.e., wandering about, or Lulu, i.e., lecherousness, lasciviousness, present themselves as interpretations. Even though the last two characteristics seem to fit Lilith well, these derivations must be ruled out because most of the leading Sumerologists tend to agree that Lila is of pure Sumerian origin.

Ki-sikil-lil-la-ke means something like: Lila's maiden, his beloved, companion or maid, while Ki-sikil-

---

1. Older spelling: Ki-sikil-lil-la

2. T.H. Jacobsen: *The Sumerian King List.* Chicago, 1939, p. 18, note 37

3. Jacobsen leans more towards the view that Gilgamesh's father was a Lilû demon

4. S.H. Langdon: *loc. cit.,* p. 358ff

5. R.C. Thompson: *Semitic Magic, its Origin and Development.* London, 1908, p. 66

ud-da-kar-ra means: the maiden who has stolen the
light or has seized the light. Incidentally, the fact that
Lilith has "seized the light" already indicates a rather
negative side to her character.

Whether a true Sumerian divine triad is concerned in this case – as many authors assume – seems
to me to be highly questionable. Against this interpretation, it must be said above all that divine triads
are of several forms. Either they contain exclusively
male figures, like the Old Babylonian trinity Anû-Bel-
Ea. Or, if a female element is included, as in the
Babylonian triad Shamash-Sin-Adad or in the Egyptian Osiris-Horus-Isis, she is always in the minority. A
trinity with two female elements has never been discovered. On the other hand, mythology does present
us with triads with three female elements such as the
Moires, Graii and Erinyes.

Against the assumption that a true triad is involved
in this instance, there is the additional fact that the
two female figures are so similar to each other that
they can scarcely be told apart. I lean more towards
the view that "the maiden who seized the light" is
nothing more than a more precise designation for
the "maiden Ki-sikil-lil-la-ke."

In Akkadian, the figures of Lilû, Lilitû and Ardat-
lili – all are equally common in the texts – correspond to these Sumerian deities or demons. Here,
too, a controversy has arisen as to whether a true
Babylonian divine trinity is involved. *Charles Fossey, B.
Meissner* and *O. Weber* seem to accept this, while *Georg-
es Contenau* refutes it.

The name Ardat-lili is interesting. *Ardatû* means a
girl of marriageable age in Akkadian. Occasionally,
the temple prostitutes at the shrine of Ishtar are
called ardatûs. In one particular magic text, it says

that the sick man has been seized by Ardat-lili, which could well imply that he has been possessed by her. Against this, it is said of *Lilitû* – although only in one isolated passage – that she has no husband. *Jacobsen,*[1] who bases himself on *Thompson,*[2] deduces that *Idlû-lili,* who is mentioned in an equally isolated – not fully substantiated – passage, is the "male counterpart of Ardat-lili"; however, this interpretation does not appear convincing to me.

Yet, if we accept the above hypothesis, according to which Lilitû and Ardat-lili are identical, then perhaps we can epitomize the latter as the more masculine side of Lilith – and thus the side of her which is closer to human consciousness.

Little is known of Lilû. It is said of him that he attempts to disturb or seduce women in their sleep by night, while Lilitû appears to men in their erotic dreams. *J.F. Jean* cites an Akkadian text, which has the following to say about Ardat-lili:

> "He, on whom Ardat-lili has cast her eyes,
> The man, whom Ardat-lili has thrown to the ground...
> Ardatû, on whom a man throws himself differently from on a woman,
> Ardatû, who has not opened herself to a man,
> Ardatû, who does not open her dress before her husband."[3]

In another text, which enumerates the lucky and unlucky days, it says of the seventh day:

> "On this day, a man should not climb up to the terrace of his house, lest Ardat-lili take him for her husband."[4]

1. T.H. Jacobsen: *loc. cit.*, p. 90, note 131
2. R.C. Thompson: *loc. cit.*, p. 66
3. J.F. Jean: *Le péché chez les Bayloniens et Assyriens.* Paris, 1925, p. 50
4. G. Contenau: *loc. cit.* Paris, 1947, p. 94

It is continually suggested that the name Lilith is connected with the Hebrew word laila, i.e., night.[1] This derivation recommends itself all the more, since Lilith is, indeed, regarded as the goddess or demon of the night. Even the Rabbis seem to have assumed such a connection, because on the one hand, they depicted Lilith as a seductive woman, and on the other, as a kind of winged nightmare being or owl-like creature. This interpretation had already been accepted in Sumer. However, from the etymological point of view, the derivation from laila does not stand up and even less so does a connection with the Assyrian lilatû, as *F. Lenormant*[2] predicates, since this does not mean night but evening.

The assumption made by *R.P. Dow*,[3] who is thinking of the Iranian lilang or lilak, i.e., dark blue, or of the Sanskrit word nila, which means indigo, is erroneous. A connection with the Indian goddess Lila, the wife of Namayana, is quite out of the question for historical reasons, because the Vishnu cult, in which these gods play a part, originated far later in history. *Maximilian J. Rudwin*'s[4] assertion that Lilith is not a proper name, but merely a collective name for female demons, is completely false.

Within Jewish mythology, Lilith – as we have ascertained – belongs to the group of demons or Shedim. If the hypotheses of *William F. Albright, Theodor H. Gaster* and others are correct, then the name Lilith

1. LVTS, Leiden, 1953, cf. Lilith
2. F. Lenormant: *La Magie chez les Chaldéens et les origines accadiennes.* Paris, 1874, p. 36
3. R.P. Dow: "Studies in the Old Testament" in BBES, Brooklyn, 1917, Vol. XII, p. 1ff
4. M.J. Rudwin: *The Devil in Legend and Literature.* Chicago & London, 1931, p. 95

already existed in the 7th century B.C. Lilith retained her Shed-like characteristics throughout the entire Jewish tradition. It is true that the original, divine character of these Shedim, did not entirely disappear in Biblical Judaism. In fact, a sacrificial altar to the Shedim existed for a long time alongside the YHWH cult, although the prophets constantly tried to combat this and to retain the priority of the belief in YHWH. This is demonstrated in particular by the passage from Deuteronomy which reads:

> "They sacrificed unto Shedim, not to God;
> To gods whom they knew not,
> to new gods that came newly up,
> Whom your fathers feared not."[1]

For the prophets, origins and the sojourn in the wilderness are the permanent ideal. Here, the YHWH image remained at its most pure. The cult of the Shedim came from the "surrounding area," i.e., taken over from the Canaanites, who for their part had learnt it from the Babylonians, who afforded the Shedim great reverence.

These Shedim are "not God"; i.e., they do not belong, or no longer belong, to YHWH's immediate circle, but they are nevertheless gods – albeit gods who, in Israel, have been demoted to the rank of demons. And here we find proof of a phenomenon which is to be encountered in the whole of comparative religious history: that with the advent of new religious convictions, the old gods were devalued. Thus, to cite but one example, under Zoroastrism, the old Iranian divinities became daevas, i.e., demons.

---

1. Deut. 32, 17

As in Canaan, so also in ancient Israel were human sacrifices offered to the Shedim:

"Yea, they sacrificed their sons and their daughters unto Shedim."[1]

Such human sacrifices were quite customary throughout the entire Orient. Even the firstborn was commonly offered as a sacrifice. Even today, the rite of "the ransom of the firstborn son" (pidjon ha'ben) by the wife – never by the husband – by means of a sum of money paid to a priest, is reminiscent of the sacrifice to the deities.

To what extent the actual sacrifice of the firstborn was carried out in ancient Israel is a matter of dispute. At any rate, the passage in the Psalm mentioned above lends itself to such a conclusion, at least for thc archaic period. The archaeological finds of *R.A. Stuart Macalister* in Gezer and *Ernst Sellin* in Megiddo also point in its favor.

The more indifferent *Se'irim* are related as well to the Shedim and to Lilith. These Se'irim, sing. Sa'ir, are mentioned in numerous passages in the Old Testament and are frequently identified with the Shedim.[2] The original meaning of the name Sa'ir is "the hairy one" and thus, by extension, the hairy scapegoat.[3] Obviously, these are archaic deities, beings in the shape of goats, similar to the fauns and satyrs. They live mainly in the wilderness, in remote places, in ruins and isolated houses, which they haunt and where they dance.[4] As with the Shedim,

1. Psalm 106, 37
2. Targum to Isa. 34, 14
3. LVTL, cf. Sa'ir
4. H. Duhm: *Die bösen Geister im Alten Testament.* Tübingen & Leipzig, 1904, p. 47ff

cult sacrifices are made to them. According to one not completely substantiated version of the Zurich Bible,[1] there was even a shrine to the Se'irim in Jerusalem. It is said of them:

> "And they shall no more offer their sacrifices unto the Se'irim, after whom they have gone a whoring."[2]

The Old Testament expression z-n-h (zoneh)[3] means something like whoring and fornicating and is specifically employed in connection with the Hierodules, the ritual temple prostitutes, an institution which found its way from Babylonia to the Canaanites and from there, in time, into the cult of Israel. The cult of the Se'irim also emerges clearly in another Biblical passage:

> "And he (King Jeroboam) ordained him priests for the high places, and for the Se'irim, and for the calves which he had made."[4]

The calves mentioned in this passage are none other than those bull gods worshipped in the Northern Kingdom of Israel after the division of the kingdom, which are identical with the Shedû. The prophets also spoke out against sacrifices to the Se'irim and *Hosea* clamored indignantly:

> "Is there iniquity in Gilead?…
> They sacrifice to the Se'irim in Gilgal."[5]

Numbered with Lilith among the Shedim and Se'irim is the desert god Azazel, to whom the scape-

1. II Kings 23, 8
2. Levit. 17, 7
3. J. Grasowski: *Milon shimushi le'sapha ha'ivrith.* Tel Aviv, 1937, cf. z-n-h
4. II Chron. 11, 15
5. Hosea 12, 11

goat laden with the sins of the people is sent by the high priest on the Day of Judgement.[1] The majority of the advocates of Old Testament knowledge are of the opinion that a pre-Yahwistic deity is concerned in this instance, who, like the other gods, has turned into a demon. Here, too, a kind of sacrificial cult is involved.

As *Neumann*[2] has shown, in most cases, this sacrificial cult serves the great mother-goddess.

At that point, the Lamashtû aspect of Lilith and the surroundings in which this originally archaic goddess lived are delimited, and we can turn our attention to other sides of her.

b) The Ishtar Aspect of Lilith

As well as her Lamashtû aspect, i.e., in addition to her role as child-stealing and child-killing demon and fearsome, devouring mother, Lilith exhibits a completely different characteristic. This other trait – which first appeared at a later date and which Lamashtû lacks almost completely – is her role as a goddess who leads men astray and seduces them. It is personified far more in another Babylonian goddess, *Ishtar*. Since, in Babylonian mythology, this goddess is virtually the prototype of the great seductress, we may also speak of an Ishtar aspect of Lilith.

In contrast with Lamashtû, Ishtar is not a clear-cut, sharply-defined personality. She is much vaguer, much more enigmatic, and has acquired different features depending on the region where she was worshipped. She, too, has aspects of the great moth-

1. Levit. 16, 5ff
2. E. Neumann: *The Great Mother*. Princeton & London, 1955, p. 147ff

er-goddess, but as queen of heaven she is totally the
opposite of the chthonic Lamashtû. Above all, however, throughout the entire Orient, she is the goddess of sensual love, lust and seduction. As a result,
she is the tutelary goddess of prostitutes and above
all of the temple prostitutes – the Hierodules – who
serve her cult. Lilitû, too, is described in a Babylonian text as a temple prostitute of Ishtar. This particular characteristic is already to be found in older,
Sumerian texts, in which it says[1] that Inanna – who
corresponds to the Babylonian Ishtar – has sent the
beautiful, unmarried and seductive prostitute Lilitû
out into the streets and fields in order to lead men
astray. This is why Lilith is also called "the hand of
Inanna."

The Hierodules who serve Ishtar are almost always
called ishtaritûs, i.e., the women who belong to Ishtar. On the other hand, Ishtar herself is called qad-
ishtu, i.e., the sacred prostitute. In ancient Israel, the
temple prostitutes were called qedeshot, i.e., holy
women. Originally, the Hebrew word q-d-sh meant
something like isolated – specifically from the pro-
fane sphere, and belonging to a sacral one. From this
arises the secondary meaning of the word applied to
something holy.[2]

Orgiastic ceremonies often took place in the service of Ishtar. Herodotus[3] reports that in Babylon
every maiden had to give herself once in her life to a
stranger and sacrifice her virginity in return for a
sum of money. However, this was in no way considered to be prostitution, because the stranger obviously represented the god. As the stranger slept with

1. S.H. Langdon: *Tammuz und Ischtar*. Oxford, 1914, p. 74.
2. LVTL, cf. q-d-sh
3. Herodotus: Hist. I 199

her, this consummation became a *hieros gamos* (sacred wedding), in which the maiden was symbolically consecrated as the god's wife.

Another prostitute related to Ishtar is *Aphrodite Parakyptusa,* worshipped on Cyprus in particular, who whistles from her window in order to attract lovers. Such representations of the woman at the window are widespread throughout the entire Orient. Especially well known are the Phoenician ivory carvings which were discovered in Arslan Tash[1], Nimrud and Khorsabad. In Babylonia, the goddess concerned is called *Kilili mushirtu,* i.e., she who leans out of the window. Now and then, she is also called "queen of the windows."

A further parallel to the seductive prostitute is to be found in the motif of the *woman in the tower.* Here, of course, we must mention above all the figure of Helen of Troy, who was looked on in medieval popular legend and folklore as a highly ambiguous, treacherous seducer of men. This interpretation goes back to a version of the capture of Troy which is certainly not reported in *Homer* but is to be found in *Virgil.* In the Aeneid, it says that:

> "At night, when the Greeks had withdrawn, Helen held an orgy in the castle with the Trojan women: she carried a torch in her hand so that the Greeks could see its light as a signal in the distance and thus would attack the city."[2]

1. J Gray: *Mythologie des Nahen Ostens.* Wiesbaden, 1969, p. 69; J. Thimme: "Phönizische Elfenbeine in Karlsruhe" in *Antike Welt. Zeitschrift für Archäologie und Urgeschichte.* Feldmeilen, 1973, Vol IV, p. 23
2. Virgil: *Aeneid* VI 517

This Helen of Troy appears to have been worshipped later as a goddess. *Gilles Quispel* reports that:

> "during excavations in Samaria, the statue of a standing goddess was uncovered, holding a torch in her right hand: as could be established from the presence of the attributes of the Dioscuri, it was a statue of Helen, who was thus found – surprisingly – to have her temple, her cult and her worshippers in Samaria."[1]

This discovery is surprising because the heterodox-Jewish Gnosis later identified Helen of Troy with another Helen, viz. the companion of Simon Magus of Samaria. According to an account by the Church Father *Ireneus*,[2] who refers in his turn to *Justin Martyr*,[3] Simon took Helen from a brothel in Tyre. She seems to have been greatly revered by Simon Magus' followers as a "holy prostitute" and "fallen Sophia." *Pseudo-Clement* says of this Helen, who in the view of Simon's followers was an incarnation of Helen of Troy, that, as she:

> "... was in a tower, a large crowd gathered to see her and surrounded the tower on all sides. But it seemed to all the people that she showed herself to the crowd through every window." [4]

This looking out of the turret window corresponds to the whistling at the window or the leaning out of the window and has always been commonly regarded as an invitation to men to let themselves be seduced by the woman concerned.

A further parallel of the Ishtar aspect is found in German medieval folklore. *A. Wuttke* points out that

1. G. Quispel: *Gnosis als Weltreligion.* Zurich, 1951, p. 62
2. Ireneus: Adv. haer. I 23, 2ff
3. Justin: Apolog. 26, 3
4. Pseudo-Clement: Recognit. II 12

Wotan's wife, Freya, later became Hulda or Mother Holle, who lives with her owl on the Hörselberg. In the folk song about Tannhäuser, she eventually becomes the Lady Venus and the Hörselberg becomes the Venusberg. Here the Lady Venus tries to seduce men and subjugate them to her service.

Let us return to the Babylonian Ishtar. Along with her reputation as prostitute and seducer of men, Ishtar was ritually worshipped throughout the whole of the Orient as queen of heaven and was known by the name Ata, Anat, Astarte or Ashera. As such, she was also known in ancient Israel, because the prophet *Jeremiah* laments:

> "The women gather wood, and the fathers kindle the fire, and the women knead their dough, to make cakes to the queen of heaven, and to pour out drink offerings unto other gods."[1]

A great number of pictorial representations on reliefs and Babylonian cylinder seals show the goddess naked, generally in the company of her two sacred animals, the lion and the dove. It seems that such small Ishtar figurines were to be found in every Babylonian house. Perhaps the teraphim or household gods[2] referred to in the Bible are also Ishtar figures, in addition to the "strange gods"[3] which are also mentioned.

Ishtar's role as prostitute and seductress is most clearly expressed in the Gilgamesh epic.

By means of her irresistible beauty and her manifold persuasive charms, the goddess is continually able to seduce gods, demigods, men and even ani-

1. Jer. 7, 18, cf. 44, 17
2. Gen. 31, 19
3. Gen. 35, 4

mals, and then to harm them. Only Gilgamesh manages to elude her clutches, because he sees through her intentions. Indeed, he even dares to call the goddess a common streetwalker:[1]

> "Gilgamesh opened his mouth to speak
> And said to the princely Ishtar:
> What must I give you (as payment for prostitution),
> if I take you?
> Do you need ointment for your body or do you
> need garments?
> Do you lack bread or nourishment?"

Then he pours scorn and derision over the goddess:

> "An oven are you, which cannot (prevent) ice…
> An unfinished door, which cannot keep out winds
> and blasts!
> A palace, which shatters the hero."

Then he enumerates all the goddess' love affairs:

> "Because you loved the colorful bird,[2]
> You struck him, you broke his wings,
> Now he sits in the forests calling 'kappi' (my wing)!
> Because you loved the lion, the all-powerful,
> You dug him graves, seven and yet again seven.
> Because you loved the docile horse,
> You lashed him, goaded him and whipped him,
> Drove him for twice seven hours.
> Because you loved the shepherd, the herdsman,
> Who constantly baked ash cakes for you
> Who daily slaughtered kids for you
> You struck him and turned him into a wolf.

1. A. Schott & W.v. Soden: *Das Gilgamesch-Epos.* Stuttgart, 1958 (table 6)
2. A. Ungnad: *Die Religion der Babylonier und Assyrer.* Jena, 1921, p. 80, translates this as "the shepherd" instead of "bird"

Because you loved Inshullanû, who tended
                                   your father's palms,
Who constantly brought you baskets full of dates,
Who daily made your table resplendent –
You raised your eyes to him, you went to him:
My Inshullanû, ah let us enjoy your strength!
And let your hand be outstretched, let it touch our na-
kedness."

When the gardener tried to elude the goddess' amorous advances, she turned her dark side to him:

"You struck him, turned him into a stunted creature[1]
And you also allowed him to live in exhaustion."

Gilgamesh concludes with great bitterness: "And were you to love me, you would do the same to me."

Now it could be objected that the motif of enchantment and transformation into an animal belongs more in the symbolic sphere of the fearsome mother. This problem will be examined in a later chapter.

2) The Arslan Tash Inscriptions and the Burney Relief

a) Arslan Tash I

In 1933, in Arslan Tash in northwest Syria, the *Comte du Mesnil du Buisson*[2] discovered an inscribed limestone plaque, which is now in the Archaeologi-

---

1. A. Ungnad: *loc. cit.*, translates the passage thus: "You struck him, turned him into a bat"
2. du Mesnil du Buisson: "Une Tablette magique de la Région du Moyen Euphrate" in *Mélanges syriens offerts à René Dussaud*. Paris, 1939, Vol. I, p. 421ff

cal Museum in Aleppo. According to *Albright*,[1] the text dates from the 7th or 8th century B.C. It contains an incantation text written in the Canaanitic (or: Hebrew, Aramaic or Phoenician) language and in Assyrian quadratic script, against a winged goddess or – according to another interpretation – against night-demons. The plaque has a hole through its upper end. *Albright* assumes from this that it was hung up as a protective amulet in the house of a woman who was about to give birth. It is unlikely that it would have been hung around the neck of the woman or her newborn child, because it is far too big. As well as the inscription, three figures are depicted: on the front, a *winged sphinx* (alternative interpretation: *a winged lion*) with a human head and a pointed helmet, below which is a *she-wolf with a scorpion's tail,* which is on the point of swallowing a naked child. The back depicts a *marching god* in Assyrian dress with a double axe and a short sword. On his head is some kind of turban with a lily, the significance of which is disputed.

The text itself has given rise to complex problems of epigraphy, Semitic linguistics and etymology, which I can only consider in passing. The greatest difficulties in conjunction with a precise interpretation of the text arise from the general lack of vocalism in Semitic scripts, so that words can take on quite different meanings according to which vowel is inserted. This lack of vowels is, incidentally, the reason why it is not always possible to state with certainty whether a singular or a plural is involved.

1. W.F. Albright: "An Aramaean Text in Hebrew from the seventh Century B.C." in BASOR, New Haven, 1939, p. 5ff

The translation of the text by *du Mesnil du Buisson* plainly contains a large number of errors. However, since then, several new and somewhat improved translations have appeared. Shortly after the first translation, *Auguste Dupont-Sommer*[1] published a new version, but this is not reliable either, because the author handles the text in a rather arbitrary manner. As a result, his conclusions, however illuminating they may be in certain respects, frequently just do not stand up and are rejected by numerous writers.

Other translations appear to be more accurate and reliable. Among these belong first and foremost those by *Albright*[2] and *T.H. Gaster*.[3] However, neither is free from speculative hypotheses. Later, *Harry Torczyner*[4] (Tur-Sinai) produced a version which, while differing completely from the previous translations, has the defect of a too limited consideration of the historico-religious comparative material. The recently published translation by *Wolfgang Röllig*[5] again follows those of *Albright* and *Gaster*.

Since the translations by *Albright* and *Gaster* agree in all the essential points but differ fundamentally from *Torczyner's* version, I am citing extracts from each which are most relevant to our problem.

1st translation: T.H. Gaster

"Incantation. O you flying goddess,

1. A. Dupont-Sommer: "L'Inscription de l'amulette d'Arslan Tash" in RHR, Paris, 1939, Vol. CXX, p. 133ff
2. W.F. Albright: *loc. cit.*
3. T.H. Gaster: "A Canaanitic Magical Text" in OR, Rome, 1942, Vol. XI, p. 41ff
4. H. Torczyner: "A Hebrew Incantation against Night-Demons from Biblical Times" in JHES, Chicago, 1947, Vol. VI, p. 18ff
5. W. Röllig: "Die Amulette von Arslan Tash" in *Neue Ephemeris für Semitische Epigraphik.* Wiesbaden, 1974, p. 17ff

O S-s-m bn P-d-r-s-a,
Sa, you god,
And o lamb-strangler (strangler of lambs):
The house I walk into,
Do you not walk into.
And the courtyard I enter,
Do you not enter.

O you who fly in (the) darkened room(s),
Be off with you this instant, this instant, Lilith.
Thief, breaker of bones."

2nd translation: H. Torczyner

"Incantation against the Ephata demons.
The oath of S-s-m bn P-d-r-s-a
Take the oath. And say to the
Strangler: the house I walk into,
Do you not walk into.
And the courtyard I enter,
Do you not enter.

To the Ephata demons in the room shadowed in
darkness
Be off, terrifying ones, terrors of my night.
You have washed with olive oil and he has gone."

Commentary:

Comparison of the two translations points up the difficulties with which epigraphy is confronted in this instance. They are evident in particular in the two lines which are of specific interest to us.

Just as Babylonian magic texts always begin with the word *Shiptû*, i.e., incantation, here the word l-h-s-t (lachashat) introduces the actual text. Originally, the word meant something like "to whisper," since such magic texts should only be recited in a whisper. L-h-s-t is the actual terminus technicus that introduces the incantation itself. Parallels are to be found in both Hebrew and Aramaic literature. In Babylonia, the corresponding expression shiptû or mamashtû also means to whisper, to murmur softly.

As concerns the term *Ephata* (alternative reading: Aphta) used in the text, the two translations differ widely from each other. Difficulties arise because it is not possible to establish with certainty whether this word is an Aramaic participle (flying) or a Hebrew noun (darkness). It is also impossible to decide definitely whether the incantation magic is directed against *a single* flying goddess or demon or against *all* night-demons. *Gaster* holds that Ephata or Aphta signifies a more precise description of a goddess. He derives the name Ephata from the Hebrew oph, which means something like "to fly." That is why Ephata is translated by *Albright* and *Gaster*[1] as "the winged one" or "the flying one," and by *Herbert Donner* and *W. Röllig*[2] and also by *Frank M. Cross* and *R.J. Saley*[3] as "the flyer." On the other hand, *H. Torczyner*[4] rejects this etymological derivation from oph. He traces the word Ephata back to the Hebrew noun epha, which means darkness or night.

Controversial opinions have arisen as well over the interpretation of the three figures. According to *Albright*, whose views are supported by *W. Fauth* and others, the gods or demons depicted on the plaque

1. T.H. Gaster: *loc. cit.*
2. H. Donner & W. Röllig: *Kanaanäische und aramäische Inschriften.* Wiesbaden, 1966, p. 44; W. Fauth: "S-s-m bn P-d-r-s-a" in ZDGM, Wiesbaden, 1971, Vol. CXX, p. 229f
3. F.M. Cross & R.J. Saley: "Phoenician Incantations on a Plaque of the Seventh Century B.C. from Arslan Tash in Upper Syria" in BASOR, New Haven, 1970, p. 42ff
4. H. Torczyner: *loc. cit.*

are invoked one after the other in the incantation text. This school believes that the winged sphinx corresponds to the "flying goddess," the she-wolf devouring the child corresponds to the "strangler," whilst S-s-m bn P-d-r-s-a is the marching god. Against this, *du Mesnil du Buisson* and *Dupont-Sommer* believe that a god called S-s-m is P-d-r-s-a's tutelary god, while *Gaster* concludes that P-d-r-s-a is a place name – though this cannot be the case, because S-s-m is clearly described as a son of P-d-r-s-a.

There is no agreement, either, about the purpose of the pictorial representations. The custom of recording gods' or demons' names and likenesses is widespread throughout the entire Orient. Whether the sight of their own image is supposed to frighten the devils and induce them to fly away, as some authors wish to believe, seems questionable to me. Probably a more obvious deduction is that the god or demon, seeing his portrait and his name on the plaque, fears that he has been identified. Since name and portrait are expressions of personality, knowledge of these is supposed to offer humans protection against the demon's machinations. In the case of helpful gods, writing down their names equates with calling on them for assistance. Drawing his likeness is a display of the power of the tutelary god.

The following word h-n-q-t, which can be read as either haniquta or hanuqita, is the most crucial word of the entire text. Its primary meaning is nothing more than the act of strangulation, but it has been applied by almost all authors to Lilith and therefore has been translated logically as "the strangler," which is correct in this context. In Assyrian, hanaqû means to strangle, to throttle. The same meaning is found in Aramaic and Ethiopian.[1] The only cause for controversy is whether a singular or plural word is involved in the text. From the grammatical point of view, both standpoints can be justified.

Albright and *Gaster* are agreed in equating the next word a-m-r with imer, i.e., lamb, and translate it thus, so that the relevant phrase in the text can be rendered as "lamb-strangler." Although the term imer for lamb is somewhat unusual and rare, it is possible to justify this interpretation. The translation "lamb-strangler" might also correspond with the parallels from Arabic quoted by *du Mesnil du Buisson,* according to which the female demon mentioned in certain Arabic mystic sources is called Karina hanuq-al-amal, i.e., ram-strangler. A similar description is given in some *Ugarit texts*[2] of the ilt-h-n-q-t-m, i.e., the strangling goddess. There are some further parallels in Syriac manuscripts published by *Hermann Gollancz.*[3] In Codex B a "mother who strangles boys" and in Codex C a "mother who strangles boys and girls" are mentioned.

The expression "the strangler" has become the established term for Lilith since the discovery of Arslan Tash I. Previously, in the variants first edited by *Myhrman* of a text which was later edited by *James A. Montgomery,* "the strangler" is not even mentioned. Instead, Lilith was named directly.

In comparative religious history and mythological research, there exist whole series of parallels for the

1. LVTL, cf. h-n-q
2. W. Fauth: *loc. cit.*, p. 51
3. H. Gollancz: The Book of Protection being a Collection of Charms, now edited for the first time from Syriac MSS. London 1912, p. 68 & 84

term "the strangler," to which *Gaster*,[1] above all, has drawn attention. For example, he tells of an incantation spell employed by the Hittites, in which a woman called Hatiyah invokes a female demon *Wisuryanza*. According to him, the Hittite word visurya corresponds literally to the Akkadian hanaqû or the Hebrew chaniquta and also means "the strangler." In this incantation spell, a picture of the goddess is taken to the seashore, where it is sprinkled with clear water. Since a similar magic rite against Lamashtû is described in the Labartû texts, a relationship between the two images cannot be denied.

However, the term "the strangler" is to be found most frequently in the Aramaic magic texts,[2] where repeated mention is made of the chaniquta, who "kills children in their mother's lap." *Montgomery* confuses the term chaniquta with aniquta or "necklace spirits," which doesn't make any sense.[3]

In a Greek magic text, published by *Richard Reitzenstein*,[4] a witch called *Baskania* or *Baskosyne* is mentioned. She is said to be a strangler who appears in many different forms (polymorphe strangalia).

While the term strangler is not disputed, the next word, a-m-r, is translated by *Torczyner* not by imer but by emor. This is supposedly an imperative form of the verb a-m-r, which means to talk, say, speak, order.[5]

The following magic formula is also of interest:

1. T.H. Gaster: "The Child-stealing witch among the Hittites" in SMSR, Bologna, 1952, Vol. XXIII, p. 134ff
2. J.A. Montgomery: ARIT, Philadelphia, 1913, p. 238 (bowl 36) & p. 146. (bowl 7), also p. 154 (bowl 8)
3. H. Torczyner has drawn attention to the correct version
4. R. Reitzenstein: *Poimandres. Studien zur griechisch-ägyptischen und frühchristlichen Literatur.* Leipzig, 1904, p. 295ff
5. LVTL, *loc. cit.*, cf. a-m-r

"The house I walk into, do you not walk into,
And the courtyard which I enter,
Do you not enter."

It seems that this demand was a widespread, ste-reotyped formula, spoken during the incantation against demons who milled around the threshold of the house, *Henri F. Lutz* has published a similar Baby-lonian text:

"You should not approach my body,
You should not walk in front of me,
You should not follow me.
Where I stop, you should not stop,
Where I sit down, you should not sit down.
You should not enter my house,
You should not cast a spell on my house.
You should not place your feet in my footprints.
Where I go in, you should not go in,
Where I enter, you should not enter."[1]

However, this line, in which Lilith is mentioned either by supposition or in fact, has given rise to the greatest controversy. While *Gaster* chooses to read it as:

"Be off with you this instant, this instant, Lilith,"

Torczyner translates it as:

"Go away at once, at once, terror of my night."

These wide differences of interpretation are possi-ble because our text unfortunately does not contain the word *Lilith* but merely *Lili*. *Albright* and *Gaster,* and *du Mesnil du Buisson* before them, are all of the

---

1. H.F. Lutz: *Selected Sumerian and Babylonian Texts.* Philadelphia, 1919, p. 32; similarly C. Fossey: *La Magie assyrienne.* Paris, 1902, p. 201

opinion that a defective spelling is involved, in which the *th* has been lost. On the other hand, *Torczyner* considers lili or leli to be a possessive form of the abbreviation lajil from the customary laila, i.e., night, and thus translates the phrase as "my night." On top of that, *Gaster* reads the word p-m as p-a-a-m, whereas *Torczyner* translate it as p-o-e-m, i.e., terror.

This passage's reference to Lilith is translated by the various epigraphers in different ways. For example, *Dupont-Sommer:*

"Chase away, chase away the Lilin."[1]

He, too, adopts a defective spelling, in which he replaces the supposedly missing letter not with a *th* but with an *n* – like other writers before and after him. However, Lilin is nothing but the plural of the singular noun Lili.

Other writers translate it as:

"Go past, step by step, Lilith,"[2] while *Cross* and *Saley*[3] lean more towards *Torczyner's* translation and thus make it:

"Go away now, now, night-demons."

From the grammatical standpoint, both translations are equally justifiable. The latter two writers also differ from *Torczyner* in that, as with *Albright* and *Gaster,* they adopt a defective spelling and add an n, so that the word reads as Lilin. In this, they – like *Salo W. Baron*[4] before them – are of the completely incorrect opinion that Lilin is the commonly used plural

1. A. Dupont-Sommer: *loc. cit.*, p. 133ff
2. H. Donner & W. Röllig: *loc. cit.*, p. 44
3. F.M. Cross & R.J. Saley: *loc. cit.*, p. 42ff
4. S.W. Baron: *A Social and Religious History of the Jews.* Philadelphia, 1958, Vol. II, p. 19

of Lilith, although *I. Lévi* had pointed out long since that:

> "Lilin est et ne peut être qu'un pluriel masculin... Le pluriel de lilith serait liliatha... il en résulte, que les Juifs connaissaient à la fois des lilin et une lilith."[1]

This conclusion is correct in so far as Lilin can never be a plural of Lilith. However, *Lévi* is mistaken in his opinion that the Jews knew only one single Lilith. Clearly, he was not yet acquainted with *Montgomery*'s recently-published texts. In these magic texts, as in various Mandaean sources – which were, however, only published at a later date – a plural of Lilith is established without further comment, in that many kinds of Liliathas are mentioned here.

According to *Gaster,* the expression m-b-z-t employed in our textual passage means something like thief, and thus nothing more nor less than child-stealer in this context. The interpretation is borne out by the subsequent lines, in which an imminent birth is spoken of. This view is shared by *Albright* and others, whereas *Torczyner* disputes it and attempts to give the passage a totally different reading.

The term p-h-z-t (pachazat) means "crusher or shatterer," according to *Gaster,* implying the breaking of bones. The expression is also found in the Labartû texts,[2] on which *Gaster* bases himself, where Lamashtû is described as the sword – alternatively, the dagger – that splits open the head. According to *Fossey,*[3] it is also said of Uttukû, the demon who is close to Lamashtû, that he splits open men's heads.

1. I. Lévi: "Lilit et Lilin" in REJ, Paris, 1914, Vol. LXXVIII, p. 20
2. D.W. Myhrman: *loc. cit.*, p. 155
3. C. Fossey: *loc. cit.*, p. 397

Fritz Pradel[1] mentions a demon, in certain medieval texts, who splits open the heads of men whom he attacks, and a child-stealing witch in *Egyptian magic papyri* is referred to as a "breaker of bones."

As regards the expression "in the darkened room" or "in the room shadowed in darkness," *Gaster*[2] has pointed out that this term is employed in Akkadian speech as the most usual designation for "the demon's house" (bit assakû). In any case, darkness seems to be part of the essence of the winged goddess or the night-demons.

Lamashtû and Lilith, too, are closely connected with darkness and night. Lamashtû is known as the "darkener of daylight," and in Sumerian, Lilith is the maiden who has seized the light. In an Egyptian magic text, the child-stealing witch is addressed thus: "You, who come in the darkness." In one of the Aramaic magic texts, it is said of Lilith, likewise, that she comes during the darkness. The *Talmud*[3] also states that a man should not sleep alone in a house (alternative translation: in an isolated house) in case he is attacked by Lilith. Finally, *Gaster*[4] has pointed out that the common Arabic word for a demon, namely djinni, is etymologically connected with the word for darkness.

With philological precision, *Torczyner* has attempted to support his interpretation by numerous linguistic parallels and references to Jewish literature. In contrast, *Albright* and *Gaster* have consulted a great deal of material from general religious history and

---

1. F. Pradel: *Griechische und süditalienische Gebete, Beschwörungen und Rezepte des Mittelalters.* Giessen, 1907, p. 20
2. T.H. Gaster: *loc. cit.*, p. 49
3. BT: Traktat Sabbat 151b
4. T.H. Gaster: *loc. cit.*, p. 49

comparative mythological research, which, for the most part, *Torczyner* disregards. But precisely these historico-religious parallels are, in my opinion, so convincing that – together with more recent specialists in Semitic epigraphy such as *Donner* and *Röllig*, for example – I prefer to side with the view of these two authors.

If the opinions of *Albright* and *Gaster* should indeed prove to be correct, then the winged goddess (Ephata or Aphta) really is related to Lamashtû and identified with Lilith. Both are recognized as child-stealing, winged goddesses. In the case of Lamashtû, this is apparent from the Labartû texts:[1]

> "May you fly away with the birds (alternatively, with the bird) of the heavens."

It is also said of her that she has "Zu's feet," and in Sumer Zu is the name for the storm petrel. Her birdlike character emerges clearly from the Sumerian version of the Gilgamesh epic published by *Kramer*.[2] The *Talmud*[3] also mentions the "wings of Lilith."

However controversial the versions and interpretations of the Arslan Tash I's inscription may be, one thing can be stated with certainty: it is an archaic incantation text directed against the winged goddess Lilith or against the demons of the night. By means of this incantation, the goddess should be prevented from entering the house of those people who are at risk from her.

All observations connected with the various translations mentioned above result in a context which, in my opinion, comes close to concluding that what is

---

1. D.W. Myhrman: *loc. cit.*, p. 155
2. S.N. Kramer: *loc. cit.*, p. 2
3. BT: Traktat Erubin 18b

involved here is in all probability an apotropaic magic text, directed against a winged goddess who appears to be identical with Lilith. The decisive factor for this hypothesis is the term "strangler," which is not questioned by any writer and which has become the commonly accepted designation for Lilith in later Jewish and non-Jewish tradition.

b) Arslan Tash II

At the same time as the inscription of Arslan Tash I, Comte *du Mesnil du Buisson* discovered a further inscribed limestone plaque, which in all probability dates from the same period as the first. In 1971, he published the text jointly with *André Caquot*.[1]

Here, too, a magic and incantation text against an unknown demon is involved. This demon himself is shown in a picture alongside the inscription. In his left hand, he holds two human legs, while half the head and the remainder of the body have already been swallowed by him, exactly like the she-wolf with the scorpion's tail from Arslan Tash I.

Like its predecessor, this second inscription also presents some epigraphical problems. All the same, it can be said that the viewpoints of the various researchers are not as widely divergent in this instance as they were in the case of the first inscription. Also, up till now, only a few epigraphical specialists have commented on this.

The contents of the incantation text are irrelevant for our problem. Only the beginning of the text is of interest to us. It, too, begins with the stereotyped

1. A. Caquot & du Mesnil du Buisson: "La seconde Tablette ou 'petite Amulette' d'Arslan Tash" in *Syrie*. Paris, 1971, Vol. XXXXVIII, p. 391ff

formula: l-h-s-t (lachashat), i.e., incantation, invocation. However, the god or demon invoked in this case is neither the winged goddess, nor a "strangler," nor a marching god. The demon – of whom we do not even know if it is male or female – is designated in this case as m-z-h (mazach). This strange name is of interest for our problem because – if it should turn out to be a female figure – it probably refers to a Lilith-like creature, even if the text refers neither to a flying goddess nor to Lilith herself by name.

Commentary:

The interpretation of the name m-z-h has not yet been satisfactorily resolved. However, it seems fairly certain that *Caquot*'s derivation of the word from the Hebrew mazah, i.e., to spray, or zehi, i.e., to sparkle, cannot possibly be correct. Both *Gaster*[1] and *Röllig*,[2] who first interpreted the inscription, point to a connection with the word m-z-o (mazo) cited in the Old Testament.[3] Certainly, the precise explanation of this word presents considerable difficulties, because it is a hapax legomenon and, as a result, parallels with the rest of Jewish literature are not applicable. The name m-z-h which appears in the passage in Deuteronomy is a so-called status constructus of a verb m-z-h which does not appear anywhere else and is used here in connection with the noun r-a-a-b, i.e., hunger. Clearly, this is a more detailed description of the condition of a people in the grip of hunger. This verb or its corresponding status constructus has been

---

1. T.H. Gaster: "A Hang-Up for Hang-Ups. The second Amuletic Plaque from Arslan Tash" in BASOR, New Haven, 1973, p. 18ff
2. W. Röllig: "Die Amulette von Arslan Tash" in *Neue Ephemeris für Semitische Epigraphik*. Wiesbaden, 1974, Vol. II, p. 28
3. Deut. 32, 24

translated in different ways by the various translators. *E. Kautzsch* and *C. Weizsäcker* translate it as "emaciated," *Torczyner* as "gaunt," *W. Gesenius* as "languishing, tired out," *E. König* as "drained" and *W.L. Holliday* with the corresponding "exhausted." In addition, *Röllig*[1] cites some parallels from the Akkadian, in which m-a-z-u-m and m-a-z-a-u-m mean something like "to squeeze out," which accords to a certain extent with the other translations. *Gaster*[2] takes passages from the Aramaic and the Syrian, in which the corresponding word means to drain or to drink dry. Accordingly, this author believes that a demon is involved in this instance which, "like the Lamia or stryx of classical folklore, drains the blood and bone marrow from its victims." In this connection, he points to the well-known, medieval amulet text of the meeting of Lilith with the prophet Elijah. To the prophet's question: 'Where are you going?' Lilith replies:

> "I am going to the woman's house and to the child she is carrying,
> to take it from her, to drink its blood, to drain the marrow from its bones and to devour its flesh."[3]

From this, it is obvious to this author that the devil concerned must be none other than Lilith, even though Lilith is not mentioned by name.

If *Gaster*'s hypotheses can really be proved correct, then the identification of m-z-h with Lilith cannot be ruled out. However, his interpretations are not convincing – in contrast with the parallels in Arslan Tash I. Against his interpretation, there is above all the

1. W. Röllig: *loc. cit.*, p. 30
2. T.H. Gaster: *loc. cit.*, p. 20
3. J.A. Montgomery: ARIT, p. 258 (bowl 42)

fact that it cannot be stated with any certainty whether the demon concerned really is a female being. As a result, the exact interpretation of this text must remain open for the time being.

c) The Burney Relief

In this connection, we can point to a pictorial representation of a winged goddess, whose iconographic interpretation has become the cause of numerous controversies among archaeologists and art historians. It concerns a reproduction – which appeared for the first time in the Illustrated London News of 13th June 1936 – of a previously completely unknown terra-cotta relief named after *S. Burney*.[1]

The relief shows the erect figure of a naked goddess of exceptional beauty. She has two huge wings and excessively long bird's feet with the talons of a bird of prey. The goddess wears a tall turban coiled round her head, the meaning of which has not yet been fully clarified. She stands on two lions which face in opposite directions and is flanked by two realistic-looking night owls which have exactly the same wings and feet as the goddess herself. In her hands she holds two strange objects, of which only part has been preserved. *Henri Frankfort*[2] interprets them as "ring and staff," which in his opinion are "the well-known attributes of the gods." Researchers like *D. Opitz*[3] and *Contenau*[4] have not expressed an

1. Cf. cover picture
2. H. Frankfort: "The Burney Relief" in AfO, Berlin, 1937/39, Vol. XII, p. 129f
3. D. Opitz: "Die vogelfüssige Göttin auf den Löwen" in AfO, Berlin, 1936/37, Vol. XI, p. 353; D. Opitz: "Die Probleme des Burney Reliefs" in AfO, Berlin, 1937/39, Vol. XII, p. 269ff
4. G. Contenau: *loc. cit.*, p. 102

opinion on the question of interpretation, while *Elisabeth D. van Buren*[1] is convinced that the figure is that of a winged Ishtar.

There are no controversies as regards the age and origin of the relief. As has generally been accepted, it is of Sumerian origin and appears to date from the so-called Isin Larsa period, i.e., some time around 1950 B.C. A similar terra-cotta was discovered by *van Buren*[2] in the Louvre. The goddess – also naked – wears a similar turban wound round her head and has the same wings as that on the Burney Relief. She, too, has the feet of a bird and her legs are feathered from the knees downwards. The two owls are missing from this relief and in place of the two lions, the goddess stands on two ibexes or wild goats, which again face in opposite directions. Finally, some fragments of two clay reliefs were uncovered in Babylonia. These depict a winged goddess from the waist downwards to below the knee. She stands on two lions whose heads can be made out quite clearly. For the rest, though, this relief is in poor condition. As in the Paris relief, here, too, the owls are missing.

That owls were not unknown in Sumer is shown by the discovery of a black hematite figure from Sumer.[3] Ibexes, too, were obviously not unknown in that country, which was crisscrossed by mountains. However, the Berlin owl is highly stylized in comparison with the Burney Relief and does not show the finely-worked details of the owl from London. *Van Buren*[4]

1. E.D. van Buren: "An Enlargement of a Given Theme" in OR, Rome, 1951, Vol. XX, p. 60ff
2. E.D. van Buren: "A further note on the Terra-cotta Relief" in AfO, Berlin, 1936/37, Vol. XI, p. 354ff
3. F. Hahn private collection, Berlin
4. E.D. van Buren: *loc. cit.*, p. 357

has put forward the hypothesis that the goddess on the Burney Relief is an Ishtar figure. In support of this interpretation, she points in the first place to the presence of the two lions, which are known to belong – together with the dove – to the animals sacred to Ishtar. She also cites a liturgical text translated by *Langdon*,[1] in which it says that Ishtar flies "over the heavens." However, a number of serious objections must be raised against this hypothesis:

1) It is correct that lions belong among Ishtar's cult animals, as emerges from numerous illustrations in her work on Mesopotamian clay figurines.[2] This is equally clear from various well-preserved Babylonian cylinder seals. A seal-roll from the P. Morgan Library, New York,[3] depicts a naked Ishtar on a chariot drawn by a winged, fire-spitting lion and in which stands the erect figure of a god (Adad or Enlil?). On a cylinder seal from the Oriental Institute, Chicago,[4] the goddess stands beside a lion. We also know of similar seal-rolls and reliefs from Assyria, from the sixth to eighth centuries B.C.[5] Against all this, however, there is the objection that lions do not belong exclusively among *Ishtar*'s cult animals. In Egypt, the lion is the animal sacred to Sachmet. *Frankfort*[6] has pointed out that, in the Babylonian-Assyrian culture group, lions are sacred to other deities, such as Ningirsu and

---

1. The text was not available to me
2. E.D. van Buren: *Clay Figurines from Babylonia and Assyria.* London, 1930, Figs. 130 & 131
3. J. Gray: *loc. cit.,* p. 18
4. J. Gray: *loc. cit.,* p. 28
5. K. Sälzle: *Tier und Mensch, Gottheit und Dämon.* Munich, 1965, p. 352f
6. H. Frankfort: *loc. cit.,* p. 135

Shamash. Lamashtû also has a connection with lions, as the Labartû texts clearly indicate.[1]

However, the presence of the two lions cannot serve as an argument that a depiction of Ishtar is concerned in this instance, because the parallel Parisian goddess stands on two ibexes, which are not considered to be animals sacred to Ishtar.

2) It is true that a series of winged male and female demons exists within the Sumerian-Babylonian culture group. Pictorial representations of a winged Ishtar are not known, however. A winged goddess from Yasilikaya is known from Hittite sources. *Margarete Riemschneider*[2] has interpreted her as a winged Ishtar, but she is much more likely to be a winged Sausga. Incidentally, no Ishtar figures have so far been discovered in which the goddess has the feet of a bird with the talons of a bird of prey. And this is also true of the Sausga.

3) The main objection to *van Buren*'s hypothesis stems from the two night owls. Owls, too, do not belong among Ishtar's cult animals. Owls are most definitely night creatures and would, therefore, be far more suitable for a goddess who carried out her deeds at night. Although Ishtar has connections with the evening star, she nevertheless has no links with owls as a consequence. And so, they would be far more suitable for Lilith, who is, of course, a goddess of the night. For this reason, *Erich G. Kraeling*[3] is also convinced that Lilith must be concerned – an opinion which is shared by *Frankfort*.[4] On the other hand,

---

1. D.W. Myhrman: *loc. cit.*, p. 148f
2. M. Riemschneider: *Die Welt der Hettiter.* Stuttgart 1954, pl. 42
3. E.G. Kraeling: "A unique Babylonian Relief" in BASOR, New Haven, 1937, p. 16ff
4. H. Frankfort: *loc. cit.*, p. 135

Frank[1] asserts "to interpret her as Lilitû (about whom we know next to nothing, by the way) is naturally completely unproven and unprovable." He, too, assumes that an Ishtar figure is involved, although he is in no way able to prove this interpretation. *Gaster*[2] is of the opinion that the goddess of the Burney Relief is none other than the winged goddess of the Arslan Tash I inscription. Insofar as she can be identified with Lilith, his opinion may be said to corroborate *Kraeling*'s thesis.

As regards winged creatures from the Babylonian-Assyrian culture group, two possible parallels present themselves for consideration.

Most of the gods and demons in Babylonian mythology – for example, the Uttuke group – do not only possess wings[3] but also "Zu's feet," i.e., bird's feet.[4]

Of the winged deities, we should mentionPazuzû and Lamashtû.

Pazuzû is a half human, half animal creature, with a dog's head and a man's body.[5] His feet are covered with birds' feathers and end in the talons of a bird of prey.[6] However, he has to be ruled out because he appears as a male god in almost all the texts. Let us, rather, consider Lamashtû, whose bird-like character emerges from the Labartû texts. Incidentally, there are magic texts with instructions to make a "portrait

1. C. Frank: *loc. cit.*, p. 30, note 5
2. T.H. Gaster: "A Canaanitic Magical Text" in OR, Rome, 1942, Vol. XI, p. 46
3. C. Frank: *loc. cit.*, p. 14, note 1
4. E. Ebeling: *Tod und Leben nach den Vorstellungen der Babylonier.* Berlin & Leipzig, 1931, p. 5
5. S. Moscati: *Geschichte und Kultur der semitischen Völker.* Zurich, 1955, pl. 8; Gray: *loc. cit.*, p. 27
6. S.H. Langdon: *loc. cit.*, p. 371

of Lamashtû" equipped with feathers.[1] Whether a clay figure or an amulet is involved is not clear from the text. *Frank,*[2] who refers to a work by *A. Falkenstein,*[3] cites a magic text in which there is supposedly a reference to Lamashtû's "eagle's talons." This would fit the passage cited by *Thureau-Dangin*[4] according to which Lamashtû has a bird's feet.

But even the assumption that Lamashtû is the goddess on the Burney Relief cannot be upheld. The goddess on our relief has a human head which is not in the least terrifying but extremely attractive, even seductive. In contrast, it is said of Lamashtû that she has the "head of a lion" and a "terrible appearance." At all events, the goddess of the Burney Relief must be a goddess of the darkness or the night, as is confirmed by the presence of the two owls.

For these reasons, we can almost certainly assume – along with *Kraeling* – that a pictorial representation of a winged Lilith is involved here.

3) Lilith in the Bible and Talmud

Only one passage in the Old Testament mentions Lilith. In the prophet Isaiah's vision of the destruction of the enemies of Zion – especially Edom – it says:

"And thorns shall come up in her palaces,
nettles and brambles in the fortresses thereof;
and it shall be an habitation for jackals,
and a court for owls.
The wild wolves of the desert shall also meet with the

1. D.W. Myhrman: *loc. cit.*, p. .155
2. C. Frank: *loc. cit.*, p. 13f
3. C. Frank: *loc. cit.*, p. 14
4. F. Thureau-Dangin: *loc. cit.*, p. 161

hyenas,
And the Sa'ir shall cry to his fellow;
Lilith also shall rest there,
And find for herself a place of rest."[1]

Commentary:

Whereas in illustrations originating from Sumer and Babylon, Lilith was a goddess closely connected with Lamashtû and Ishtar, in Biblical literature she – together with other spectral figures – has already become a colorless spirit of the desert. However, it was generally assumed that everyone knew of her existence.

Gaster has advanced the rather daring supposition that the male Lili can also be found in the Book of Isaiah. Because in this, it says:

"Ve'ha'elilim kalil jachaloph."[2]

The controversies that have arisen from this ambiguous passage require us to make a short critical analysis of it. The verse is usually translated:

"And the idols he shall utterly abolish."[3]

The prefix *ve* means something like "and," while *ha* is the definite article, both in the singular and the plural. The noun *elilim* is a plural, which is derived from the singular El, i.e., god. Its use in this context has an overtly pejorative implication and means "idols." Any connection with the wind god Elil – as has been assumed – may be ruled out because his name should correctly be spelt Enlil. Elilim is generally translated as "nullity." In their translations of the

1. Isa.: 34, 13f
2. Isa.: 2, 18
3. Translation from the King James' Bible

Bible, *Torczyner* speaks of "nothingness" and *Martin Buber* of something driven by "non-godliness," *Hans Wildberger* in his commentary on Isaiah translates the word aptly by "vain beings." Elilim is also used in the sense of idols in other Biblical passages, especially in Isaiah[1] and Ezekiel.[2]

The verb *jachaloph* is the future form of the third person singular of the word ch-l-ph and means: to move past, to go past. In this sense, it is employed in connection with a stream which flows past,[3] or a wind which blows overhead.[4]

The translation of elilim and jachaloph is not under dispute. It is equally certain that jachaloph refers only to kalil and not to elilim, because this would be completely impossible from the grammatical point of view. What is controversial, however, is the meaning off the word *kalil*. If we follow the almost universally accepted translation, the word is derived from the Hebrew kol, i.e., complete, full, entire. It is used in this sense in several passages in the Old Testament.[5]

But the commonly accepted Biblical translations of this passage are, admittedly, not very satisfactory.

Accordingly, *Gaster*[6] proposes dividing the word kalil into: ka, i.e., like, like a, and lil, which he takes to be a defective spelling of Lili and translates as follows:

"And the idols – like a Lili which flutters past."

1. Isa.: 10, 10
2. Ezek.: 30, 13
3. Isa.: 8, 8
4. Isa.: 21, 1
5. Judg.: 20, 40; Ezek.: 16, 14
6. T.H. Gaster: *loc. cit.,* p. 50 note 1

But even this translation fails to provide a satisfactory solution, since the hypothesis is highly speculative and is refuted by most students of the Old Testament.

The passage cited from Isaiah presupposes that it was generally known who Lilith was. Nothing more is said about her nature, her appearance and her activities. Later Biblical commentators were the first to describe her as a female demon,[1] as an animal that howls in the night, or as a bird which flies about.[2] In their interpretations, they seem clearly to have been influenced by the Talmud. Incidentally, the Rabbis, who did not know the etymology of the word Lilith, associated this with the word laila, or with its short form, lajil, i.e., night.

In Talmudic literature, however, a new element makes an appearance: Lilith as a seductive woman. Up till now, the Lamashtû aspect was the only one to appear, but from this point onwards, the Ishtar aspect comes more and more into play. In the Talmud, too, Lilith is portrayed as a completely negative figure.

That she was perceived as such a dangerous and demonic figure in the Talmudic-Rabbinic tradition has both historical and psychological bases. In the first place, it is connected with the patriarchal attitude of Talmudic-Rabbinic Judaism, in which the feminine was always perceived as something threatening. As a result, in Judaeo-Christian, Western cultural development, the feminine was not only devalued but also, in consequence of a marked defensive

1. S. Jizchaqi: Raschi to Isa. 34, 14
2. D. Qimchi: Redaq to Isa. 34, 14

attitude, virtually demonized. We will discuss the psychological consequences of this attitude later.

Incidentally, both the *Talmud* and the contemporaneous narrative *Midrashim* have little to say about Lilith. However, her demonic character is clearly expressed in various passages, e.g.:

> "R. Jirmija ben Eleazar said: All the years in which Adam, the first man, was excommunicated (meaning the 130 years between the death of Abel and the birth of Seth, in which he kept away from Eve), he begat ghosts, devils and Lilin."[1]

In another passage in the Talmud, it says:

> "R. Jirmija ben Eleazar said: They (which means the people who tried to build the Tower of Babel) were divided into three groups... Those who said: Come, we will arise and make war (against God), were (turned into) apes, ghosts and Lilin."[2]

The commentator *Salomo Jizchaqi*[3] says about Lilin that they had a human body but also had wings.

In a Talmudic treatise, reference is made to a female demon called Agrat, daughter of Machlat, who is related to Lilith and who also attempts to strangle men. Many authors identify her with Lilith:

> "Do not go out alone at night. Because the teachings say: Do not go out on the night of Wednesday or the Sabbath (which are supposed to be unlucky days), because those are the times when Agrat, daughter of Machlat, roams about in the company of 18 myriad angels of death, all of whom are associated with strangling."[4]

1. BT: Traktat Erubin 18b
2. BT: Traktat Sanhedrin 109a
3. S. Jizchaqi on Sanhedrin 109a
4. BT: Traktat Pessachim; Midrash Num. rabba 12, 1

Among the passages which depict Lilith as a seductive woman is a text which speaks of Lilith's long hair and wings.[1]

Another text says:

> "R. Chanina said: One should not sleep alone in a house (alternative translation: in an isolated house), because whosoever sleeps alone in a house will be attacked by Lilith."[2]

In later Rabbinic tradition, Lilith plays the role of a succuba, who visits Adam and has children by him on each occasion, and she is also referred to in a passage in the Syrian *Book of Baruch*, an apocryphal work published around the time of Christ:

> "I will call on the sirens of the sea,
> The Liliths, who come out of the wilderness,
> And on the Shedim and Tannim of the forests."[3]

The sirens referred to in this passage are related to the Striges of Graeco-Roman mythology. Like them, they have the head of a seductive woman, while their body takes the form of a bird or, in other interpretations, that of a fish. According to legend, the Sirens were the daughters of the river-god Acheloos and the nymph Kalliope. Even today, there is a belief in Greece:

> "that the Sirens of Parnassus lure sailors in danger from a storm by means of their bewitching songs. In the hope of imminent salvation, the unhappy ones steer in the direction of these sweet sounds. But the closer they believe themselves to be to the deceptive

---

1. BT: Traktat Nidda 24b; Traktat Erubin 100b
2. BT: Traktat Sabbat 151b
3. R.H. Charles: *The Apocrypha and Pseudepigrapha of the Old Testament.* London, 1913, Vol. II, p. 485

voices, the farther away these move, and so they are tempted to sail on and on until eventually they are drowned."[1]

4) The Aramaic Magic Texts

Some of the most important sources for understanding the Lilith myth are, without doubt, the Aramaic magic texts. First of all, they reflect opinions as expressed in Jewish popular belief in Babylonia. The vast majority of these inscriptions were discovered in Southern Babylonia during archaeological investigations undertaken by the University of Pennsylvania. Since then, similar inscriptions have been found in a great diversity of areas in the Middle East. At an even earlier period, *Sir Austen Layard*[2] discovered several magic texts in Babylon and Niniveh and found them to contain incantation texts against Lilith. The texts published in 1913 by *Montgomery*[3] come from the inside of bowls discovered in the ruins of houses in a Jewish settlement in Nippur. Only a few of the bowls had inscriptions on their outside as well.

The date of manufacture of these bowls and of their inscriptions has not yet been definitely established. According to *Montgomery* and others, it might well have been in the 6th or 7th centuries A.D.

Both *Jakob N. Epstein*[4] and *Torczyner* have pointed to a large number of errors and misinterpretations in *Montgomery*'s translation. However, despite numer-

---

1. B. Schmidt: *loc. cit.*, p. 132
2. A.H. Layard: *Discoveries in the Ruins of Niniveh and Babylon*. London, 1853, p. 512f
3. J.A. Montgomery: ARIT, Philadelphia, 1913, p. 13ff
4. J.N. Epstein: "Glosses Babylo-Araméennes" in REJ, Paris, 1921, Vol. LXXIII, p. 27f & MAIT, 1922, Vol. LXXIV, p. 40ff

ous shortcomings in that version, these magic texts do form an important contribution to the understanding of the Lilith myth.

The fact that the majority of the inscriptions were engraved on the inside of the bowls has given rise to the assumption that these used to be filled with a liquid – perhaps water or wine – which the person who was bewitched had to drink. By this means, the efficacity of the incantation was reinforced and the texts themselves were absorbed, so to speak. According to *Ethel S. Drower*, it is

> "… an old Mandaean custom, in times of plague and other diseases, to bury two bowls next to the threshold of the house or beside someone's grave, one upside down on top of the other, the insides of which carry incantations against demons of illness, ghosts of darkness, Liliths, etc., together with curses against those who bring sickness and misfortune."[1]

Drower[2] assumes in this connection that the bowls imparted healing powers against demons when water was drunk from them.

However, recent Mandaean research has abandoned the view that these bowls were used to drink some kind of liquid, and today the consensus is that they served to entrap the evil spirits.[3]

Up till now, the problem has remained unsolved. Why exactly were *bowls* used in this incantatory magic, and what was the reason for them being *buried* in the earth on each occasion?

---

1. E.S. Drower: MII, London, 1937, p.25
2. E.S. Drower: *loc. cit.,* p. 318, note 4
3. J.A. Montgomery: ARIT, p. 41, cf. H. Pognon and H.O. Hilprecht; R.C. Thompson: *Semitic Magic.* London, 1908, p. IVf

The motif of the *bowl* or vessel is an archaic, widespread, i.e., *archetypal* symbol, which played an important part in medieval alchemy above all. The alchemical transformation took place in the alchemist's vessel, which had to be "hermetically" sealed. It is true that neither the Aramaic nor the Mandaean magic bowls are sealed, but two bowls were frequently buried with their open ends together.

Jung gave an illuminating explanation of the use of bowls or vessels in his Tavistock Lectures. In these, two illustrations of vessels were reproduced, which had been painted by a patient whose diagnosis was uncertain. The first picture showed a vessel which contained drawings of completely unconnected objects. Because of the "break-lines" in these drawings, *Jung* diagnosed the pictures as expressing a form of schizophrenia, which did indeed prove to be the case. According to Jung,

> "A vessel is an instrument for containing things. It contains for instance liquids, and prevents them from getting dispersed. Our German word for vessel is *Gefäß*, which is a noun of *fassen*, that is, to set, to contain, to take hold of. The word *Fassung* means the setting, and also, metaphorically, composure, to remain collected. So the vessel in this picture indicates the movement of containing in order to gather in and to hold together. You have to hold something together which otherwise would fall asunder."[1]

So it can be said, analogously, that the magic bowls also contain something – namely, the incantation text – that should not be allowed to escape, since this would carry certain dangers with it.

---

1. C.G. Jung: "The Tavistock Lectures" (1935), Lecture V, Discussion, in *The Symbolic Life*, CW Vol. XVIII, Princeton, 1976, p. 176

Furthermore, since almost all the bowls are completely circular, another motif is added: on the one hand, it signifies a protective circle, on the other, the mandala, which points to total unity. As with the hermetic vessel, nothing must be allowed to escape from the mandala. Likewise, the incantation text, too, must not be allowed to escape in case it causes damage.

The *burying* of the bowls is easier to understand. It concerns the expression of an archaic magic attitude of mind: the dangerous or the evil is banished out of sight, thus rendering it almost nonexistent. Such banishment ceremonies are known to exist among numerous peoples throughout the whole of religious history. Among the Jews, on the Day of Atonement, the scapegoat laden with the sins of the people is sent to Azazel, who lives in the wilderness. In medieval German popular belief, illnesses were frequently buried.

Psychologically speaking, banishing evil out of sight signifies nothing more nor less than a driving out, a wish-not-to-see, which for primitive people meant the same as not existing.

By means of banishment into the bowls, through the force of the spoken word, the demons were compelled to stop interfering with people, cattle, houses and all the other possessions of the bewitched person – and to vanish.

Magic practices as employed in Babylonia and among the Hittites are either completely missing or only play a secondary role. Apart from magic invocations, many bowls contain texts from the Old Testament, e.g., from Deuteronomy or the Psalms. At the beginning or, more frequently, at the end of the ritual, we read each time that the demons

should be "bound and sealed" or that they should
be "sealed, bound and invoked in the four corners
of the house." Frequently, the exorcism is carried
out "in the name of the great prince Michael,"
meaning the archangel of that name. Through him,
the demons are "bound with seven magic formulae
and sealed with seven seals."[1] Now and then, as further support, the archangels Gabriel and Raphael
were invoked, or "Hermes, the great master," and
also "Abraxas, the protector of good and destroyer
of evil spirits,"[2] as well as Metatron, the "Lord of the
Countenance."[3] Here and there, the Patikhras, i.e.,
ghostly figures, are called on for help. The word is
supposed to come from Middle Persian (Pehlevi)
and may be connected with the Pairikas, i.e., beautiful, seductive, female demons who bewitch men.[4]

In later amulet texts, Adam and Eve, the first father and first mother, are invoked against Lilith –
together with three particular angels who are named
exclusively in connection with such incantations
against Lilith.

The demons mentioned in the Aramaic magic
texts are generally not referred to by name. In most
cases, they are described simply as "the killer," "the
demon," "Satan" or "the robber." Only one demon is
regularly referred to by her name: Lilith, although
all female demons are described as Liliths (liliatha).
Depending on the activity concerned, a more precise
term is added to the proper name. The name generally used for Lilith is "the strangler" (chaniquta or

1. J.A. Montgomery: ARIT, p. 138 (bowl 5)
2. J.A. Montgomery: ARIT, p. 146 (bowl 7)
3. C.H. Gordon: Aramaic and Mandaic Bowls in AO, Prague, 1937,
   Vol. IX, p. 93 (Text L)
4. A. Kohut: *Über die jüdische Angelologie und Dämonologie in ihrer
   Abhängigkeit vom Parsismus.* Leipzig, 1866, par. 86

chanuqita), exactly as in the far older inscription of Arslan Tash I.

The demons who are invoked cause both illnesses of the body and disorders of the soul. However, magic formulae exist that are supposed to cure barrenness in women or prevent miscarriages.[1] Some texts contain a love spell, by means of which a husband's cooling love may be won back.[2]

The analogy between the Aramaic and Mandaean magic texts and the Babylonian incantations does not seem to me to be as great as is assumed by *Heinrich Zimmern,* who sees in them evidence of the "continuing influence of Babylonian demonological ideas in Judaism."[3] Despite numerous shared ideas, the differences between them are, nevertheless, highly pronounced.

The Lilin and Liliths invoked in these texts are conjured to leave the bewitched person and his home and possessions alone. Thus, all "demons, devils, Satans and Liliths" who live under the lintel of the door or who lurk on its threshold are forced to take themselves off.[4] Because wherever there is some kind of entrance, demons lie in wait. Above all, Lilith is warned not to appear at night in dreams nor during the slumber of daytime.[5]

Two of the Nippur bowls contain an almost identical text. And a further, analogous text has been published by *Cyrus H. Gordon,* part of which says:

1. J.A. Montgomery: ARIT, p. 168 (bowl 11)
2. J.A. Montgomery: ARIT, p. 178 (bowl 13) and p. 213 (bowl 28)
3. E. Schrader: *Die Keilinschriften und das Alte Testament* ed. H. Zimmern. Berlin, 1902/03, p. 463
4. J.A. Montgomery: ARIT, p. 141 (bowl 6)
5. J.A. Montgomery: ARIT, p. 154 (bowl 8)

"This bowl is intended to seal the house of Gevanai, so that the evil Lilith may flee from him, in the name of 'El, who has scattered' the Liliths, the male Lilin and the female Liliths, the shelanitha and the chatiphata, the three, the four and the five. Naked shall you be driven away, unclothed, with your hair loose and streaming behind your back."[1]

Commentary:

The three, the four and the five refer less to Lilith's companions and more to different types of Lilin and Liliths. The two strange terms shelanitha and chatiphata (alternative spelling: chataphita) are definite terms of insult, which appear not only on these two bowls but also in later Oriental Jewish texts. Their translation remains a matter for speculation to this day. *Montgomery* translates them as "hag and ghoul."[2] Hag means something like witch, while the word ghoul is the specific Arabic word for a demon, somewhat similar to the Arabic djinni. *Montgomery* believes as well that there is a connection between shelanitha and the Arabic word shi'lat, which also means witch. In addition, a derivation from the Assyrian shulû, i.e., spectre, must be taken into consideration.[3]

But all these etymological derivations are questionable. Probably, the name shelanitha is an example of a corrupt spelling. *Scholem*[4] has conjectured that the original spelling of the word was talanitha, which is highly possible from the epigraphical point

1. C.H. Gordon: *loc. cit.*, p. 93 (Text K); cf. JR Montgomery: ARIT, p. 154 (bowl 8) and p. 190 (bowl 17)
2. J.A. Montgomery: ARIT, p. 155 (bowl 8) and p. 190 (bowl 17)
3. J.A. Montgomery: ARIT, p. 157 (bowl 8)
4. G. Scholem: *A New Interpretation of an Aramaic Inscription* in JG, Philadelphia, 1965, p. 88

of view, since the letters SH and T share a certain similarity. In support of his interpretation, *Scholem* calls on an Aramaic text published by *Dupont-Sommer*,[1] in which a talanitha is clearly mentioned alongside other demons. This term is translated by *Dupont-Sommer* as "La Ténébreuse" and by *Scholem* as "The Shade."

On the other hand, *Gordon*[2] had already published a text from an Aramaic magic bowl in which a talanitha is also mentioned. *Gordon,* too, assumes this to be a corrupt spelling, but, in complete contrast, conjectures that the correct form should be shelanitha – without, however, being in a position to give a more detailed explanation for it.

Fewer difficulties arise from the translation of chatiphata. The word means nothing more nor less than robber, predator, grabber, exactly like the Babylonian ahhazû. These are terms which appear time and again in connection with Lilith.

Montgomery, and *Gaster* after him, pointed out in this connection that the ritually unclean bird *Tachmas*[3] mentioned in two places in the Bible is also translated as chatiphata in one of the Aramaic translations of the Bible – namely, in the Targum Onkelos. The word Tachmas is derived from the root ch-m-s, which means something like to use or employ force.[4] It is possible, therefore, that there are links between Lilith and chatiphata on the one hand and

---

1. A. Dupont-Sommer: "Deux Lamelles d'Argent à l'Inscription Hébréo-Araméenne trouvées à Agabeyli" in JKF, Heidelberg, 1950/51, Vol. I, p. 201f
2. C.H. Gordon: *loc. cit.,* p. 93 (Text K)
3. Levit.: 11, 16; Deut.: 14, 15
4. LVTL see ch-m-s

Tachmas on the other – but this is not completely proven.

Since the finds in Nippur, similar magic bowls have been unearthed in many different areas of the Near and Middle East, with the result that the science of bowls has developed into a specialist field of epigraphy. A large number of bowl texts have been published and annotated by *Gordon, Julian Oberman* and *Javier Teixidor*. One passage from an Aramaic bowl published by *Gordon* runs:

> "Sealed and sealed again (are) the house and threshold of Adaq, son of Mahlapta, for his wife Mamai, against all evil poltergeists, demons, monsters and Liliths, against all wind demons and mischief makers, so that they do not come near the house and threshold of Adaq, son of Mahlapta... They are sealed with three rings and again with seven seals."[1]

It is the ring and seal that give special emphasis to the incantation and are supposed to have a deterrent effect on the demons.

The Nippur bowl number 8 contains an especially impressive and solemn incantation text:

> "You must never again appear in his house, nor in her room, nor in her bedchamber. For you should know, (Lilith), whose father is *Palhas* and whose mother is *Pelahdad,* that *R. Josua ben Perachja* has proclaimed a ban against you. I conjure you by (the name of) Palhas, your father, and Pelahdad, your mother: A divorce certificate has come to us from heaven. In this is written some information and a warning for you, for you, in the name of *Palsa-Pelisha.* You, Lilith, male Lili and female Lilith, shelanitha and chatiphata, you are ban-

---

1. C.H. Gordon: "Aramaic Incantation Bowls" in OR, Rome, 1941, Vol. X, p. 120ff (Text 3). Cf. also E.M. Yamauchi: "Aramaic Magic Bowls" in JAOS, New Haven, 1965, Vol. LXXXV, p. 512

ished... You must never appear again, either in the dreams of night or during the slumber of the day. For you have been sealed with the seal of El Shaddai, the seal of the house of Josua ben Perachja, and through the seven that are before it. You, Lilith, male Lili and female Lilith: I conjure you by the severity of Abraham, the rock of Isaac, the Shaddai of Jacob. YH is his name, YH his memory. Your divorce certificate, delivered by the holy angels... I tear out the evil stranglers and their evil Liliths. Do not ever return to them from this day forward. Amen."[1]

Commentary:

The above-mentioned text contains a few gaps, which, however, are not important for our understanding of it. We cannot state with certainty whether the magic spell applies to the husband or to his wife or to both. The devils and Liliths are conjured not to appear by night or by day. It is said that they not only appear in dreams and visions but that they also create them. And so they appear by night and during the noonday rest. This particular time of day is believed by many races to be an especially dangerous, even ill-omened period. Harmful noonday demons (Taharirin) are also to be found in Jewish literature. In Greek mythology, midday is the time when fauns and satyrs seize hold of people, if they are unfortunate enough to find themselves out in the open.

What makes this text especially interesting is the divorce ritual it contains. The man bewitched by Lilith behaves exactly as if he were married to her. However, this affords Lilith certain legitimate, marital rights. The object of the divorce is to deprive her of these rights. The divorce ceremony is carried out

1. J.A. Montgomery: ARIT, p. 154 (bowl 8)

exactly in accordance with a genuine legal divorce. In each case, the name of the wife's father is given in the divorce certificate.[1] In our example, in fact, the names of both of Lilith's parents are given. However, the meaning of their names is not known.

R. Josua ben Perachja – a teacher of the Talmud who lived in the first century B.C. and who is constantly referred to in the Talmud – is regularly quoted as the great authority in the field of demonic incantations and exorcisms.

The possibility of divorce originally belonged exclusively to the man, under prevailing Jewish law – according to which, the wife is the husband's property. A judicial authority cannot issue a divorce decree. A wife is entitled to ask for a divorce only in a few precisely specified circumstances e.g. in the event of maltreatment, if the husband refuses to maintain her properly, or if he forces her into a dishonorable occupation. However, since the Rabbinical conference in Worms in 1040 A.D., a wife's rights have been clearly prescribed.[2]

The divorce is carried out by means of the delivery of a certificate, which must be written according to highly specific rules. The husband hands his wife the divorce letter with the words: "Here is your divorce letter, accept it and be separated from me from now on and free for all other men."

It is the divorce certificate that really determines the final separation of the married couple. In our example, it was sent in the name of Palsa-Pelisha, i.e., by him "who separates and has separated."

---

1. M. Cohn: JL, Berlin, 1928, Vol. II, see get (= divorce letter)
2. M. Cohn: JL, Berlin, 1928, Vol. II see marital law

The Rabbis merely have the authority "to bind and free" demons. But for a legally valid divorce from a demon, an additional, divine authority was required. And so our text states that the divorce certificate was sent "from heaven."

A further magic text from a bowl discovered in Iran has been published by Gordon:

> "Be bound and sealed, all you Shedim, Daevin and Liliths, with the heavy, strong and powerful chains with which Sison and Sisin were bound. The evil Lilith who leads the hearts of men astray, who appears in dreams during the night and in visions by day, who burns and destroys[1] like a nightmare, who seizes and kills boys and girls, youths and maidens: Defeated is she and sealed out of the house and threshold of *Bahram-Gusnasp,* son of *Ishtara-Nahid,* through the talisman of Metatron, the great prince, who is called 'the great healer'... He defeats Shedim and Daevin, black arts and powerful magic spells... Defeated are the black arts, the powerful magic spells, defeated are the bewitching women, their witchcraft, their sorcery, their curses and incantations. Banished are they from the four walls of the house of *Bahram-Gusnasp,* son of *Ishtara-Nahid.* Defeated and downtrodden are the bewitching women, defeated on earth and in heaven. Bound are the works of their hands. Amen."[2]

Commentary:

This is actually a Jewish text, but one that is meant for the non-Jewish followers of Zoroaster. This is already obvious from the names Gusnasp and Nahid.

---

1. According to G. Scholem, what is involved here is not Lilith's "burning and destroying," but rather her "rise and fall." (Written communication from Prof. Scholem)
2. C.H. Gordon: "Two Magical Bowls in Teheran" in OR, Rome, 1951, Vol. XX, p. 306ff

According to *Gordon,* Gusnasp means something like a young horse, while Nahid – the Iranian name for Ishtar – was a common name for women. The Daevin referred to in the text correspond to the Daevas of Zoroastrism and the Devs of Mandaeanism. They are demonic beings in the service of Angru Mainyu.

The *Metatron* mentioned in the text is the "Lord of the Countenance," the high master of the angelic hosts, who plays an important role in early Jewish mysticism (the so-called Merkaba mysticism), above all.

Since a specific type of word magic is involved in all these incantation texts, it is not to be wondered at that they continually repeat the same words and set phrases in highly similar texts, with the intention of strengthening their magic or apotropaic effectiveness.

On the one hand, the Aramaic magic texts reveal how widespread was the belief in demons – especially the belief in Lilith. On the other, they also reveal the fears that people had of this demonic figure which they truly believed to be a real, living being.

For men, Lilith is the great seductress, who "leads their hearts astray." She lures them away from their wives, exactly like the Karina in Arabic literature.

The view taken by *Montgomery,*[1] dismissing women's fears of Lilith as "most developed products of the morbid imagination of the barren or neurotic woman, the mother in the time of maternity, of the sleepless child," is one that I do not share, because it is an all-too-rational and simplified explanation. This is not a question of the "imaginings" of neurotic

1. J.A. Montgomery: ARIT, p. 77

women, but fears that all women have of Lilith. Incidentally, men, too, were similarly affected.

The fact that demons were also viewed as bringers of disaster and above all of all physical and mental disorders is connected with the archaic, magical world view which left a decisive mark on the people of that time. In the *Babylonian magic texts,* the illnesses caused by demons are enumerated. Among these are sprains to arms and legs, broken bones, and diseases of the gall bladder, liver and heart.[1] Similarly, *Egyptian magic* ascribes illnesses to the machinations of demonic beings, and the *Greek magic papyri* are full of such ideas. Similar notions are easy to find in the *New Testament,* too. In *Matthew,* devils are mentioned that cause "blindness and deaf-mutism."[2] Jesus gave his disciples power "to cast out unclean spirits and to heal all manner of sickness and all manner of disease." In the *Nippur texts,* the following are also named: plague, leprosy, strokes, and also infertility and miscarriages in women. All this is to be attributed exclusively to external causes, personified by spirits and demons.

Some of the Aramaic magic bowls also contain pictorial representations of Lilith. She is mostly depicted as naked, with prominent breasts and unbound hair that streams wildly behind her back.

5) Lilith in Gnosticism

Lilith is referred to as well in a passage in Gnostic literature, although only indirectly.

This is an amulet text which is particularly difficult to date but which most probably originated in the

1. M. Jastrow jun.: *loc. cit.,* p. 367
2. Matt.: 10, 1

17th century. It describes the encounter between Lilith and the prophet Elijah in the form of a folk legend. At the time, *Montgomery*,[1] following the example of *R. Gottheil*, who first copied down this text, assumed that an inscription from a Nippur bowl was probably concerned, since

> "… a bowl would have been a perfect place for a text of this prophylactic character."

Since then, however, it has been proved that this assumption was erroneous – because *Scholem*,[2] has pointed out that this Lilith legend was not known in earlier Jewish literature. However, since it is cited by certain specific, heterodox, non-Jewish Gnostics, it must be assumed that the legend derives from earlier, originally orally transmitted Jewish sources, since a non-Jewish origin can be ruled out. At the same time, though, these Gnostics have altered the contents of the legend to accord with their own interpretation. In this connection, *Scholem* cites the *Panarion* of the Father of the Church, *Epiphanius*, a markedly anti-Gnostic work, dating from between 375 and 377 A.D.,[3] which mainly reflects the opinion of the so-called *Barbelo-Gnosis*. In this work, the encounter between Lilith and Elijah is described as follows:

> "There came, so people say, a female demon, who stopped him and said to him: 'Whither do you go? For I have children by you and you cannot ascend (to heaven) and abandon your children.' And he replied: 'How can you have children by me, have I not lived in the ways of holiness?' She said: 'Yes, in sleep, in your

1. J.A. Montgomery: ARIT, p. 258 (bowl 42)
2. G. Scholem: "Relationship between Gnostic and Jewish Sources" in JG, Philadelphia, 1965, p. 72f
3. K. Rudolph: *Gnosis und Gnostizismus*. Darmstadt, 1975, p. 309

dreams, you were often emptied by the outflow from your body. Then I received your sperm and bore you children.'"

Elijah's encounter with the demon occurred after his journey to heaven, when the prophet had already returned to earth. Although in this version of the legend Lilith is not referred to by name, there is nevertheless no doubt that the legend must refer to her, because parallel Jewish texts mention her expressly by name. In the Jewish versions, Lilith is defeated by Elijah. However, the Gnostics have completely reversed the sense of the legend by depicting Elijah as being conquered by Lilith, with the result that he can no longer ascend to heaven. The polemical, anti-Jewish jibe that forms the basis of the Gnostic version should not be ignored.

Above all, however, Lilith is mentioned in numerous passages of *Mandaean literature*. The Mandaean religion is a specific category of the Gnostic teaching on redemption, at the centre of which – as in most Gnostic schools – lies the true "knowledge" (Gnosis), known as "knowledge of life" (Manda de Haije) in Mandaeanism, which is also personified as a kind of Redeemer figure. The main characteristic of Mandaean Gnosis is its syncretistic quality, because it contains Christian and above all Jewish elements alongside some from Zoroastrism and Mithraism. Presumably, the influence resulted less from official Judaism than from heterodox sects, in particular from the baptismal cult of the Elcasides and the Qumran community. Nevertheless, Mandaeanism, like *Markion*-influenced Manichaeism, shows itself to be markedly anti-Jewish, while also coming out against the "false religions" of Christendom and Islam. In modern Mandaean research, there exists a lengthy controversy about the pre-Christian origins of this Gnostic religion: *Geo Widengren,*[1] together with *Henri-Charles Puech* and *Karl Rudolph,* are convinced of these pre-Christian origins, but *Gilles Quispel*[2] questions them.

Mandaean is an East-Aramaic dialect, closely related to the Aramaic of the Babylonian Talmud. Nowadays, it is used by the surviving descendants of the Mandaeans, who live in Iraq and Iran, purely as a ritual language.

In Mandaean literature, too, the name Lilith is used either as a term for a specific female demon or – more frequently – as a collective name for a group of female demons, who come from the realm of darkness.

Demons play a significant part in Mandaean Gnosis and are mentioned in a large number of their canonical writings, to wit, in both parts of the *Ginza* (Sidra rabba), in the Qolasta and in the Mandaean Book of John (Drashe de malke). This last names Lilith (either in the singular or as Liliths in the plural) as the embodiment of all female demons. Together with numerous other spirits (Saharias), demons (Devs and Shidias), fiends (Hmurtas), amulet-temple- and chapel-spirits,[3] and in the company of idols, vampires, forest demons and other harmful spirits, they people the realm of darkness.[4] They are all ruled by a terrible mother-goddess, the *Qin,* the "mother of darkness," her husband *Anatan* and their

---

1. G. Widengren: "Die Ursprünge des Gnostizismus und die Religionsgeschichte" in K. Rudolph: *loc. cit.,* p. 698ff
2. G. Quispel: Book review of W. Foerster: Gnosis. A Selection of Gnostic Texts, Vol. II in Bibliotheca Orientalis, Leiden, 1975, Vol. XXXII Nr. 5/6, p. 372
3. M. Lidzbarski: GR, Göttingen & Leipzig, 1925, p. 277f
4. M. Lidzbarski: GL, p. 540

children – among whom we find her daughter *Ruha,* who rules alongside or in place of her mother, her son *Gaf,* the brother and husband of Ruha, and her daughter *Lilith-Zahriel,* more usually called simply Zahrel or Zahril. With her lover/son *Ur,* Ruha, the "mother of the seven" (planetary spirits) and the "twelve" (signs of the Zodiac), rules the realm of darkness.

The various sides of Lilith's character are expressed by specific names, just as in the Aramaic magic texts. The latter speak of a *Lilith-Taklat,*[1] who "kills boys and girls" and is described as the granddaughter of a *Lilith-Zarnai.*[2] A *Lilith-Hablas,*[3] the "eater," who strangles children, is also described as the granddaughter of Lilith-Zarnai. As such, she appears in an Aramaic exorcism text. *Guiseppe Furlani*[4] has listed further names for Lilith.

In the Mandaean Book of John, a *Lilith-Azath*[5] is mentioned, who lives with her attendant hordes in the "Sinios" i.e., the royal palace in Rome. It is said of a *Lilith-Jilath*[6] that she lives on the banks of the river Ula.

Above all, we should mention *Lilith-Zahriel,*[7] the daughter of Qin and sister of Gaf and Ruha. Her importance is already shown by the fact that she is

---

1. J.A. Montgomery: ARIT, p. 168 (bowl 11) & p. 193 (bowl 18)
2. A. Marmorstein published the same Midrash in which a Lilith-Zarnai is mentioned in Debir, Jerusalem, 1923, as did L. Ginzberg in Ha'goren, Berlin, 1923
3. C.H. Gordon: "An Aramaic Exorcism" in AO, Prague, 1934, Vol. VI, p. 467
4. G. Furlani: "Il Nomine dei Classi dei Demoni presso i Mandei" in RANL, Rome, 1954, Vol. IX, p. 407f
5. M. Lidzbarski: Jb, p. 13, note 3
6. M. Lidzbarski: Jb, p. 152
7. M. Lidzbarski: GR, p. 160

frequently referred to as "Great Zahriel" (Zahril rab-batia). However, there appears to be no connection between her and the angel Zahriel who is well-known from Jewish angelic lore.[1]

To understand the idiosyncratic characteristics of this Lilith figure, it is necessary to investigate some of the central ideas of Mandaean Gnosis.

The Mandaeans' religious ideal is moulded by *Kushta,* a concept which – according to the context in which it appears – can have different meanings. The word Kushta means, first and foremost, truth, honesty, sincerity, uprightness, and loyal behavior.[2] The Mandaeans' greatest concern is to walk in the "paths of Kushta." Because Kushta is:

> "for the Mandaeans, the embodiment of their religion, of right and truth in the behavior of the faithful to-wards the most supreme beings as well as towards each other."[3]

In addition, Kushta plays an important part in the Mandaeans' cult and rites. "To give Kushta" denotes the ritual handshake, which is associated with the fraternal kiss[4] given by the "brothers and sisters in Kushta" in the most varied circumstances. As well as this, though, Kushta appears as personified,[5] as a redeemer or savior-figure, similar to other light be-ings or Uthras. That is why Kushta must correspond to the *Asha* in the Yasnas of the Avesta. Asha, too, means truth and also appears as a personified figure.

1. M. Lidzbarski: Jb, p. 11
2. W. Brandt: *Die mandäische Religion, ihre Entwicklung und geschicht-liche Bedeutung.* Utrecht, 1899, p. 111
3. M. Lidzbarski: Jb, p. XVII
4. E.S. Drower: *The Canonical Prayerbook of the Mandaeans.* Leiden, 1959, p. 2, note 1
5. K. Rudolph: *Die Mandaer.* Göttingen, 1961, Vol. II, p. 140

As in the Yasnas, questions are put to the supreme creator-god, Ahura Mazda, so also are questions put to Asha and, in Mandaeanism, to the "beloved Kushta."[1] On the other hand, Kushta also puts questions to the more senior beings of the world of light – for example, to the demiurges *Ptahil* and his son *Jokashar* – and expects them to give both an answer and instruction on Mandaean redemption teaching's path of salvation. The answers she receives will be passed on to the faithful. Kushta is particularly suited to this role of mediator because she stands "at the gate of the worlds," i.e., on the threshold of the two realms. Thus, she is a kind of divine wisdom and – psychologically speaking – an anima in the mould of Sophia.

One of Kushta's questions goes:[2]

"Tell me, in whose womb will the child be formed? If it should be in the mother's, whose odor will it smell? Which Lilith perches on the bed of the pregnant woman?"[3]

The answer to this question is given to her by the demiurge Ptahil:

"When the child is formed, it will be taken from the father's hip and thrown into the mother's uterus. When the child develops in the mother's uterus, it will smell the odor of life. It is Lilith-Zahriel that perches on the bed of the pregnant woman."[4]

The text makes a distinction between "to form" and "to develop." The formation, i.e., moulding, of

1. K. Rudolph: *loc. cit.,* p. 143
2. M. Lidzbarski: Jb, p. 8 & 10
3. E.S. Drower: MII, Oxford, 1937, p. 57, note 7 translates it as: "beside the pregnant woman's bed."
4. M. Lidzbarski: Jb, p. 10

an individual is effected by the father, whereas further development is carried out by the mother.

It would be natural to assume that this Lilith-Zahriel is waiting for the birth of the child in order to steal it and kill it. However, such is not at all the case. To understand this particular Lilith's character, we must briefly examine the Mandaean myth of "Hibil-Ziva's descent into hell."

As do almost all Gnostic-dualistic teachings on redemption, Mandaean Gnosis believes in an upper world of light, the world of the spirit, called *pleroma,* and a lower realm of darkness, the contrasting world of matter. When the heavenly beings learned that a leader was to be born in the realm of darkness who would begin a battle against the world of light, they decided to forestall him. And so, an envoy was sent from the world of light to the world of darkness, to begin the fight against the leaders of this realm.

The chief representative of the realm of light appears under different guises, to which different terms are applied. Sometimes he is described as *mara de rabbuta,* i.e., "Lord of the Great," and on other occasions as *malka roma de nehora,* i.e., "The illustrious King of the Light." The envoy of the realm of light is either Manda de Haije himself, or more often than not, his son *Hibil-Ziva,* i.e., "radiant Abel."

Hibil-Ziva forces his way into the realm of darkness. He asks Anatan and Qin for one of their daughters as his wife. They agree. They give him their younger daughter, Lilith-Zahriel. Hibil-Ziva hopes to uncover the secrets of the realm of darkness by means of this alliance. And he succeeds in this, because he steals the three things to which the powers of the forces of the realms of darkness are linked: namely, a magic mirror, a crown and a magic pearl.

After his marriage to Lilith-Zahriel and the theft of the magic articles, Hibil-Ziva leads his wife out of the underworld and into the realm of light. Their son is the demiurge Ptahil who – in accordance with his origins – contains elements of both realms.[1]

However, with Lilith-Zahriel's ascent into the clear pleroma, a transformation takes place. In his work on the Mandaeans in Iraq and Iran, *Drower* explains that, in this myth, Lilith is no child-stealing demon. On the contrary, she is a spirit who is friendly and helpful towards the pregnant woman, "responsible for the child's well-being before and after its birth."[2]

Presumably, this transformation of a Lilith figure into a guardian angel for the mother and her child is connected to her ascent into the realm of light. The psychological aspects of this motif should not be overlooked and will be dealt with later.

With the exception of Lilith-Zahriel, however, all other Liliths are viewed as dangerous demons in Mandaeanism. The magic formula with which Hibil-Ziva can excommunicate them goes as follows:

> "Be you fettered and bound, giants of the darkness, and fettered be your bodies with the strong chains with which smiths fetter monsters. Fettered be your magic and the illusions you create. Fettered be your wives, the Liliths, the salamanders, those deformed figures that are ugly, perverted and misshapen, whose appearance and constant chattering no-one can tolerate."[3]

Another passage of the Ginza, which contains a polemical jibe at ascetic Christianity, says:

1. E.S. Drower: MII, p. 271
2. E.S. Drower: MII, p. 46f
3. M. Lidzbarski: GR, p. 154

"They (the Christians) leave their houses and become monks and nuns. They deny one another their seed, the women the men and the men the women. They deny the world their seed and their descendants. They impose fasting on their mouths, and they are put in chains (?). They keep food and drink away from their mouths and keep white fasting gowns away from their bodies. Then Liliths go to them, take sperm from them and become pregnant. They give birth to spirits and forest demons who attack human children."[1]

In Mandaean Gnosis, Lilith is known more than anything through numerous incantation texts. In a prayer in the Qolasta, a passage runs:

"Banish and drive away from me, N.N., and from those souls who have climbed down to the Jordan and have been baptized, the fear, dread and terror of all spirits, demons and Liliths."[2]

The majority of the magic texts were discovered in Kish and around the Euphrates. Others were uncovered in Nippur. Like the Aramaic magic bowls, these texts probably date from the 6th to 7th century. They were published by *G. Driver, E.S. Drower, C.H. Gordon, Mark Lidzbarski, J.A. Montgomery* and *Henri Pognon.* Later on, *Edwin M. Yamauchi* collected, annotated and re-edited them.[3]

One magic text from Iran says:

"Bound is the bewitching Lilith, who has cast a spell over the house of Zako. Bound is the bewitching Lilith with a band of iron around her head, bound is the bewitching Lilith with clamps of iron in her mouth. Bound is the bewitching Lilith, who haunts the house

1. M. Lidzbarski: GR, p. 50
2. M. Lidzbarski: "Das Qolasta" in ML, Berlin, 1920, p. 42
3. E.M. Yamauchi: MAIT in American Oriental Series. New Haven, 1967, Vol. II

of Zako, with an iron chain round her neck, with fetters of iron on her hands and blocks of stone on her feet."[1]

The Mandaean bowls also contain the occasional pictorial representation of Lilith with outstretched arms and fettered hands. Another text says:

"Bound are the Liliths with chains of lead. Bound are the male bewitching demons, bound are the female bewitching Liliths, who create hateful dreams, hallucinations, apparitions, hateful visions and hateful delusions."[2]

In a similar text, Lilith is called upon to leave, together with other demons:

"I conjure you, Lilith-Haldas, and you, Lilith-Taklath, granddaughter of Lilith-Zarnai, who lives in the house and on the threshold of Hormiz, son of Mahlapta and of Ahata, daughter of Dade, who strikes and kills and bewitches and who strangles boys and girls... O Lilith-Haldas, flee, depart, vanish from the house, the threshold, the palace and the buildings, from the bed and pillow of Hormiz. And do not show yourself to them, either in their dreams or in their visions by day."[3]

There are magic spells by women who beg for protection for themselves and their children, both born and unborn:

"Health, protection and defence for P... his body and his soul and for the unborn child and the womb of Bardesa, whose mother is the daughter of Dade. Bound are the sorcerers with fetters of iron, bound are the Liliths with chains of lead."[4]

---

1. C.H. Gordon: "Two Magical Bowls in Teheran" in OR, New Haven, 1967, Vol. XX, p. 309ff
2. E.M. Yamauchi: MAIT, p. 213 (Text 17)
3. E.M. Yamauchi: MAIT, p. 231 (Text 21)
4. E.M. Yamauchi: MAIT, p. 261 (Text 24)

In one Mandaean text, there appears a motif that plays an important part in Jewish and Arabic literature – i.e., Lilith as disrupter of marital relations:

"I will estrange the husband from his wife and with my magic I will drive her away and do her evil… I will kill the man with desire and passion… and she will bear orphans."[1]

In this connection, we must briefly look into whether Lilith is also to be found in the Gnostic-Coptic works that were discovered in Nag Hammadi, as *Quispel*[2] assumes.

All three versions of Codices II, III and IV of the *Apokryphon of John*,[3] and the corresponding report of the Church Father, *Ireneus*,[4] on the so-called Barbelo-Gnosis, mention an aeon called *Eleleth,* who could be identified with Lilith. More details about this figure – described as "The Archons' Being"[5] – are given in another Gnostic work from Codex II. Here, Norea, a daughter of Eve, begs Eleleth to help her, because she has fallen under the control of the Archons. Eleleth is "wisdom and the Great Angel, who stands before the Holy Ghost." He is sent by the latter to Norea to free her from the "hands of the lawless" (i.e., the Archons) and also to teach her about "the roots" (namely, of truth and the origins of humanity).

1. E.M. Yamauchi: MAIT, p. 297 (Text 33)
2. Written information from Prof. G. Quispel
3. M. Krause & P. Labib: "Die drei Versionen des Apokryphon des Johannes" in *Abhandlungen des Deutschen Archäologischen Instituts Kairo.* Wiesbaden, 1962, Vol. I (Cod. 11:8, 18; 9, 23. Cod. III: 14, 7. Cod. IV: 13, 1)
4. Ireneus: Adv. haer. I 29, 1f
5. W. Foerster: *The Hypostasis of the Archons in Gnosis. A Selection of Gnostic Texts.* Oxford, 1972, Vol. I, p. 49f

In these few texts, Eleleth appears as a helpful being, as a light-aeon or a divine hypostasis from the realm of light, a kind of Sophia figure. I cannot side with the hypothesis that identifies Lilith with Eleleth, because Eleleth completely lacks the characteristics that are typical of Lilith. Apart from a distant similarity between the two names, it seems to me that there is no other connection between the two figures.

Finally, we must mention that *Gordon,* who claimed to have deciphered the Linear A script of the Minoan texts from Knossos and to have identified it as a Semitic script, refers to a passage in which *La-le* – whom he identifies with Lilith – is mentioned in this work. Apart from the fact that we know next to nothing about La-le, *Gordon*'s hypothesis has also been rejected by almost all specialists in epigraphy.

6) Pseudepigraphic Writings

a) The Testament of Solomon: Obyzouth

Sometime between the third and fourth centuries A.D.,[1] a work appeared which has become known as the *Testament of Solomon.*[2] This is a pseudepigraphic work, written in Greek, which has been preserved in a revised Christian version and which, according to most authors, such as *Fred C. Conybeare,* is of Jewish origin. According to *Scholem,*[3] it must definitely date back to Judaeo-Hellenic magic ideas.

In the Testament of Solomon, the archangel Michael gives King Solomon a magic ring, which will

1. The exact dating is a matter of dispute
2. C.C. McCown: *Testamentum Salomonis.* Leipzig, 1922
3. G. Scholem: JE, Jerusalem 1972, Vol. XI, cf. Lilith

afford him protection against all demons. Solomon asks all the demons he meets for their name and for that of the angel to whom each is subject and whom each must obey.[1]

Lilith is not mentioned by name in this work. However, a figure called Obyzouth is described who is either very closely connected with her or who may even possibly be her. It is said of her:

> "And what seemed to be a woman – from her face – came to me, veiling her body and her limbs with the hair that she had loosened. And I, Solomon, said to the demon: Who are you? She said: And who are you, and why do you wish to know what I am? But if you wish to know this, then go into the royal chambers, wash your hands, seat yourself on your throne again and ask me. Then will you learn, o king, who I am.
>
> After I, Solomon, had done these things and had seated myself on my throne, I asked her and said: Who are you? She replied: Men call me Obyzouth. I do not sleep by night but go round the whole world and visit women in childbed. When I see the hour approaching, I take my place and when I spot an opportune moment, I strangle the child. If I fail, then I withdraw to another place, because I cannot pass even one single night without success… For I have nothing else to do but kill children, make their ears deaf, cause harm to their eyes, shut their mouths fast, befuddle their senses and torment their bodies.
>
> When I, Solomon, heard this, I said to her: Tell me, evil spirit, by which angel may you be rendered harmless? She said to me: By the angel Apharoph. And when women give birth, they should write my name on a piece of paper, and I will flee that place."[2]

1. J. Petroff: JE, Jerusalem 1971, Vol. XV, cf. Test. of Solomon
2. C.C. McCown: *loc. cit.*, p. 43ff

Commentary:

That a Lilith-like figure is involved is quite clear from the whole context of the passage. Even the name Obyzouth seems to point in this direction. The name itself has not yet been interpreted with any degree of certainty. But on later Graeco-Byzantine amulets, a child-stealing and child-killing demon is given the name Byza or Abouzou, which, according to *Schmidt*,[1] means something like bloodsucker. One of this demon's secret names is Gyllou (Gilû in Hebrew),[2] which in its turn is one of Lilith's mystic names.[3] In Kabbalistic literature, Obyzouth[4] is one of the secret names for Lilith.

The text clothes itself in the garb of a legendary tale. In the process, the correct *rite d'entrée* must be performed before the encounter with the demon can take place. Only then will Obyzouth divulge her name to the King and thus reveal her true being. The hero of this entire work is King Solomon, who in both Jewish and Arabic literature has always been accepted as the lord and master over all spirits and demons. *Flavius Josephus*[5] had already mentioned that Solomon had composed an incantation text intended to afford protection against demons.

Encounters between Lilith and Solomon are to be found later in the Aramaic magic texts as well as in Kabbalistic literature. There, the two harlots who lay

1. B. Schmidt: *loc. cit.,* p. 139ff
2. H.A. Winkler: *Salomo und die Karina. Eine orientalische Legende von der Bezwingung einer Kindbettdämonin durch einen heiligen Helden.* Stuttgart, 1931, p. 110
3. G. Scholem: "Lilith û malkat sheva" in: *Peraqim chadashim me'injeney Ashmedai ve' Lilith.* TZ, Jerusalem, 1947/48, Vol. XIX, p. 71
4. The Greek theta has been lost in the Hebrew texts
5. Fl. Josephus: Antiquit. VIII 11, 5

their dispute over the child before Solomon are none other than the two demons Lilith and Na'ama – the latter being frequently identified with Lilith. Lilith was also identified with the Queen of Sheba, as *Scholem*[1] has pointed out.

In the Testament of Solomon, Lilith or Obyzouth's role as a seductress of men is relegated completely into the background. Here, her exclusive function is to strangle children. However, she does not do this on her own initiative but because she was created solely for this purpose.

New to this text is a motif that appears time and again in numerous myths, fairy tales and legends: the discovery and writing down of the secret name or names of a god or demon provides protection against their destructive power. The angel Apharoph referred to in our text is none other than the archangel Raphael, who was invoked primarily against demons who brought sickness, because Raphael means: God heals. This is based on an archaic, magical idea: because the name of a god or a demon, but also of a man, or his image, is also a part of his being just like his body or his soul. In Greece, it was the knowledge of the Logoi Hekatikoi (the names of Hecate) which was supposed to afford protection against the dangerous machinations of the goddess Hecate. In Egypt, the names of the gods had to be learned correctly for use on the Day of Judgement. There, the custom was to threaten the gods continually on the basis of the knowledge of their names – a practice that was much reproved by the Church Father *Porphyrios*. Thus, in an Egyptian amulet text, the supplicant

1. G. Scholem: "Lilith û malkat sheva" in *Peraqim chadashim me'injeney Ashmedai ve'Lilith.* TZ, Jerusalem 1947/48, Vol. XIX, p. 165ff

attempts to use his knowledge of the secret names of the god concerned to compel him to give assistance:

"Afford me your mercy, for I have pronounced your 'hidden name' (to krypton onoma)."[1]

On a Coptic amulet is written:

"I beseech you by the great cherub of the fire, whose name no-one knows, I beseech you by the great name of God, whose name no-one knows."[2]

By revealing her hidden name, Obyzouth submits herself to Solomon's power. At the same time, she reveals the name of the angel whom she herself must obey. Clearly, as a result of this, the king is able to call upon the angel and thereby compel the devil to leave her victim alone.

b) *The Alphabet of ben Sira*

A further pseudepigraphic work, which, from the point of view of time, follows on from the Gnostic and Aramaic texts, is a Midrash – i.e., a story – showing Lilith in a totally new light. The passage referring to Lilith runs as follows:[3]

"The son of the king (Nebuchadnezzar)[4] suddenly fell ill. The king said to him (ben Sira): Heal my son, if you fail, I shall kill you. Immediately, he sat down and wrote an amulet in the name of *purity* and wrote on it the names of the angels responsible for healing, with their

---

1. C. Bonner: *Studies in Magical Amulets chiefly Graeco-Egyptian*. Ann Arbor, 1950, p. 23
2. J. Drescher: "A Coptic Amulet" in *Coptic Studies* in honor of W.E. Crum. Boston, 1950, p. 269
3. Alphabeta de'ben Sira: ed. M. Steinschneider fol. 23a f, Berlin, 1858
4. My brackets and emphasis

names, their images, their hands and their feet. When
Nebuchadnezzar saw the amulet, he said to him (ben
Sira): Who are they? He replied: They are the angels
responsible for healing: Senoi, Sansenoi and Semangloph.

When the Almighty – may His name be praised – created the first, solitary man, He said:[1] It is not good for
man to be alone. And He fashioned for man a woman
from the earth, like him (Adam), and called her Lilith.
Soon, they began to *quarrel* with each other. She said to
him: I will not *lie underneath,* and he said: I will not *lie
underneath* but above, for you are meant to lie underneath and I to lie above. She said to him: We are both
equal, because we are both (created) from the earth.
But they didn't listen to each other. When Lilith saw
this, she pronounced God's *avowed* name and *flew* into
the air. Adam stood in prayer before his Creator and
said: Lord of the World! The woman you have given
me has gone away from me. Immediately, the Almighty
– may His name be praised – sent three angels after
her, to bring her back. The Almighty – may His name
be praised – said to him (Adam): If she decides to return, it is good, but if not, then she must take it upon
herself to ensure that a hundred of her children die
each day. They went to her and found her in the middle of the sea, in the raging waters in which one day the
Egyptians would be drowned. And they told her the
word of God. But she refused to return. They said to
her: We must drown you in the sea. She said to them:
Leave me! I was created for no other purpose than to
harm children, eight days (after birth) for boys and
twenty for girls. When they heard what she said, they
pressed her even more. She said: I swear by the name
of the living God that I, when I see you or your image
on an amulet, will have no power over that particular
child. And she took it upon herself to ensure that, every day, a hundred of her children died. That is why we
say that, every day, a hundred of her demons die. That

1. Gen. 2, 18

is why we write her name on an amulet for small children. And when she (Lilith) sees it, she remembers her promise and the child is saved."

About the translation:

Since the ben Sira text has given grounds for various psychological speculations and interpretations, it seems to me to be necessary to examine certain relevant passages in greater detail – both from the point of view of language and from that of content.

First and foremost, it is important to say that the whole text is written in Medieval Hebrew, which, compared with the Classical Hebrew of the Bible, is less precise.

Since ben Sira wrote the amulet *"in purity,"* we may presume that his intentions were completely honorable and that he wanted nothing to do with magic practices. This was not self-evident, since such amulets have been prepared for magic purposes, by Jews and Moslems alike, up till the present day.

The word that I have translated as *"to quarrel"* is represented by *"mit'garin"* in our text. The verb's ending is Aramaic. The verb is used in the reflexive (hitpael) form of the simple, "easy" (qal) conjugation of the uncommon verb g-r-h. Both *Abraham ibn Shoshan*[1] and *Jehuda Grasowski*[2] translate it as "to fight one another" or "to begin a fight with each other." This interpretation also follows from the context of the passage.

The translation of the expression *shem ha'mephorash* is rather more difficult. In Hebrew, shem means name. The verb me'phorash is derived from the root

1. A. ibn Shoshan: *Milon chadash.* Jerusalem, 1958, cf. g-r-h
2. J. Grasowski: *Milon shimushi le'sapha ha'ivrith.* Jerusalem, 1937, cf. g-r-h

p-r-sh. It is practically uncommon in its usual form (li'phrosh). On the other hand, it is extremely well-known in its intensive conjugation (pi'el). In this form, it means something like "to explain, to eluci-date, to interpret." Thus, the corresponding noun perush means explanation. Our text uses the passive form (pu'al) of the verb, and so "me'phorash" must be translated as "avowed." All other translations that have been proposed, such as: the hidden, the excellent, the specific, the unpronounceable or the clearly pronounced name, fail to express the true meaning of the word and thus should be rejected.

In addition, the chosen translation "the avowed name" is backed up by the story that tells of Moses' encounter with God in the burning bush.[1] In response to Moses' question as to how he should tell the children of Israel in Whose name he comes, He *explains* His name by means of this expression "Ehjeh asher ehjeh," which, literally translated, means "I am that I am." In reality, this cryptic formula contains the name YHWH.

Whenever shem ha'mephorash is mentioned in Hebrew, it refers exclusively to the divine name YH-WH, and never to other divine names such as El, Elohim, Shaddai or Zebaoth.[2] In Biblical times, no-body was afraid to speak this name. And so Hosea[3] the prophet speaks of the "word of YHWH," that commanded him to take a whore as a wife; or Jeremi-ah[4] to whom "the word of YHWH came in the days of

1. Exod. 3, 14
2. A. Kristianpoller: "Gottesnamen in Talmud und Midrasch" in JL, Vol. II
3. Hos. 1, 1
4. Jer. 1, 2

Josiah." The same formula is also employed by other prophets, such as Amos or Jonah.

Only much later did the custom emerge that the high priest alone was permitted to pronounce the name of YHWH before the congregation on the Day of Atonement, on entering the Holy of Holies. *Ethel W. Vogelsang*[1] asserts of the name YHWH that "the ineffable name of God is the Tetragrammaton, which includes the feminine and masculine aspects of God." She puts forward similar assertions in connection with the divine name Elohim, when she says: "This terminology for 'God' (Elohin) is sometimes interpreted as 'El,' the male singular together with 'in,' the feminine plural. This would define God as androgynous."[2]

Her lack of understanding of Hebrew has obviously led this author to read from the text something that she had earlier projected into it. The name YHWH is the term for a definitely masculine divinity, who, from being a patriarchal desert and tribal god ("The God of the Fathers"), developed into a national god ("The God of Israel") and, later, gradually, into a more universal god. No trace of a female element is to be found in the divine name YHWH. The same is true of the divine name Elohim. The ending of the word is not Elohi*n* but Elohi*m*. The ending -im is the characteristic expression of the *masculine* plural. It is possible that the name Elohim may indeed originally have had a plural meaning. But by the time the Elohist began writing the work down, it had already acquired a singular meaning, because in Genesis it says: "In the beginning, God

1. E.W. Vogelsang: *loc. cit.,* p. 53
2. E.W. Vogelsang: *loc. cit.,* p. 49

created the heaven and the earth." Had a plural been involved, then the verse should read *Elohim barím* (pl.), not *bará* (sing.).[1] Thus it is completely absurd to speak of an androgyny of God's two names. It was only more than 2000 years after the Elohist that Provençal and Catalan Kabbalists began to speculate about a feminine side to God. In any case, this was completely unknown to the author of the ben Sira texts. The meaning of the angelic names Senoi, Sansenoi and Semangloph, who are supposed to afford protection against Lilith, is not totally clear. Like that of other divine and angelic names on amulets, the meaning of these is disputed. Thus, angelic names such as Sandalphon, Aktriel or Sephariel are mentioned, as well as Metatron, "the Lord of the Countenance" – all of whose meanings remain unclear. On the Lilith amulet, the wish "out, Lilith" is frequently found alongside the three angelic names.

Commentary:

The Alphabet of ben Sira is a medieval popular book with a pseudepigraphic character. Its exact dating is still a matter of dispute. The majority of experts believe that it was written sometime between the ninth and tenth centuries. Only *Moses Gaster*[2] is of the opinion that the work originated as early as the seventh century, which strikes me as unlikely. At any rate, it was known to the author of the Talmudic dictionary "Aruch," the lexicographer *Nathan ben*

1. Gen. 1, 1
2. M. Gaster: "Two thousand years of a charm against the child-stealing witch" in *Studies and Texts in Folklore, Magic, Mediaeval Romance, Hebrew Apocrypha and Samaritan Archaeology.* New York, 1971, p. 1008ff

Jechiel in the 11th century, and also to *Moses de León,* who lived around the middle of the 13th century, because he refers to it in a passage of his principal work, the Zohar.[1] The philosopher, *Moses de Maimon* (Maimonides), the contemporary of Moses de León, thoroughly disapproved of the book. Throughout the whole of the Middle Ages, this Midrash appeared to enjoy widespread popularity.

According to *Bernhard Heller,*[2] the work is made up of two originally quite separate sections, each containing 22 proverbs, which begin with the 22 letters of the Hebrew alphabet. The two sections were later combined, but inconsistencies occasionally result. Thus, according to one version, the three angels come down to earth and immediately begin to talk to Lilith. But in another version, the angels have to seek out Lilith, whom they eventually find in the Red Sea. In a variant text, they find her in the desert.

The first version of the Alphabet, written in Aramaic, contains stories, fables and aphorisms, whose aim is to give further clarification of the 22 proverbs. The second version contains a framework story into which the 22 proverbs are worked. In the framework story, the life story of the alleged author is outlined – his birth as the son of the prophet Jeremiah and his daughter, how his teacher teaches him the alphabet when he is only a year old. A further section tells of ben Sira's life at the court of the Neo-Babylonian King Nebuchadnezzar II, who lived around 600 B.C.,

---

1. Zohar I 34b: "In old books, we found…" clearly refers to ben Sira's Midrash, according to a verbal communication from Prof. G. Scholem
2. B. Heller: "Das Alphabet des ben Sira" in EJ, Berlin, 1928, Vol. II, p. 454ff

which ben Sira describes in great detail. This section also contains the episode that speaks of Lilith.

It is to be assumed that the Midrash was written in an Arab country, because both sections contain a series of Arabisms.

A certain difficulty in producing an exact interpretation of this Midrash arises out of the existence of more than 50 manuscripts and numerous printed versions, which partly contradict each other.[1] The most important editions are:

1) *Codex Leyden* ed. M. Steinschneider. Berlin, 1858, fol. 23a f

2) MS Leyden, contains part of the Leyden Codex but is otherwise rather more detailed

3) ed. I. Lévi. Paris, 1894, REJ, Vol. XXIX & XXX

4) ed. D.S. Löwinger & D.Z. Friedmann in *Festschrift for L. Blau.* Budapest, 1926, contains a continuation of the Leyden Codex

5) ed. M. Habermann in TZ, Jerusalem, 1958, Vol. XXVII

In more recent times, the Leyden Codex has been considered as the most reliable source, and so I have kept to this edition of the text in my translation. As regards content, it contains several divergences from earlier German texts. *Gaster* has submitted both an English[2] and a German[3] translation which have, however, shown themselves to be inaccurate. On top of this, they fail to agree with each other on several points., As a result, I have refrained from including them in this study and have instead followed the original Hebrew text.

1. Y. Dan: "Alphabeta de'ben Sira" in EJ, Jerusalem, 1972, Vol. VII, p. 547ff
2. M. Gaster: *loc. cit.,* p. 1032ff
3. M. Gaster: *loc. cit.,* p. 1252ff

The commentary follows in the chapter "Lilith and Adam: The Power Struggle," page 177.

c) The Book of Raziel

The book of Raziel is a work which, so legend has it, was given to Adam by the angel Raziel, three days after he was driven out of Paradise, and in which all the secrets of all the ages are contained. As a result, it is also called the "book of the first man." In reality, it is a pseudepigraphic work, barely a few pages in length, and forming part of a larger collectanea. Its authorship is wrongly attributed by certain experts like *Leopold Zunz*[1] to *Eleazar von Worms,* one of the so-called "pious men of Germany." In fact, these collectanea contain widely differing cosmological, astrological, mystical and magical texts, as well as fragments of texts from quite different epochs. Thus, for example, they contain the first part of the work called Ssode rezaja, whose author is indeed *Eleazar von Worms,* but also a part of the Sefer ha'razim (Book of Magic Secrets), which probably dates back to Talmudic times, in addition to extracts from works of the two Spanish Kabbalists *Abraham Abulafia* and *Josef Gikatila* and other Kabbalistic passages from *Isaac Lurja's* Jewish mysticism. The book was first published in 1701 and went through numerous reprints, because – according to Jewish popular belief of the time – it protected its owner from burning and other dangers.[2]

---

1. L. Zunz: *Die gottesdienstlichen Vorträge der Juden.* Berlin, 1832, p. 168, note a
2. Y. Dan: JE. Jerusalem, 1971, Vol. 13, cf. Book of Raziel

The Book of Raziel also contains an invocation against Lilith:[1]

> "I conjure you, *first Eve,* in the name of Him who created you and in the name of the three angels whom the Lord sent to you and who found you on the islands in the sea. You had sworn to them that, whenever you found their names, neither you nor your host would do any evil, neither you yourself, nor your hosts, nor your servants, to either this woman or her child that she has born, neither by day nor during the night, neither at the time of feeding nor at the time of drinking, neither to their head nor to their heart, neither to their 208 limbs nor to their 365 blood vessels. I conjure you, your hosts and your servants by the power of these names and these seals."

Commentary:

The text is closely related to the preceding text. If *Gaster's*[2] hypothesis that the book was compiled in the tenth century from considerably older material proves to be correct – although this is disputed by several authors – then it cannot be ruled out that the author of the Book of Raziel and that of the Alphabet of ben Sira may have used the same source independently of each other. However, in view of the difficulties in arriving at an exact dating for both works, it is perfectly possible that the author of the one knew and made use of the other – although this means that the question of which came first must remain open for the time being.

Although this text uses the term "first Eve" for Lilith, she appears here exclusively in her guise of a

1. Sefer Raziel: ed. Amsterdam, 1701, p. 43 B
2. M. Gaster; *loc. cit.,* p. 1008ff

terrifying mother. Her first appearance as a seductive anima is yet again in Jewish mysticism.

7) Lilith in Folk Legend

As the centuries passed, the Lilith myth continued to develop and to enter the folklore of widely differing regions. What was involved was a series of legendary tales, which, for a long time, were handed down orally and were only written down at a much later date. Nevertheless, it is possible to trace these Lilith legends back to their origins – at least, to a certain extent. They are part Graeco-Byzantine and part Jewish texts, which were widely circulated, as is shown by the existence of Coptic, Ethiopian, Armenian and Syrian legends. But these legends reached the West, too, and so versions also exist in the Neo-Greek, Southern Slav and Russian folklores. However, it would be wrong to attribute the wide circulation of this motif exclusively to its *migration*. That the tale itself is to be encountered almost everywhere and that the manner of its presentation is somewhat primitive both lead to the assumption that, in this instance, an *archetypical* motif is involved and that it became constellated as a result of migration.

All these legends involve highly embellished tales in which a child-stealing and child-killing female demon encounters some saint or other who vanquishes her because he extracts from her the secret of her mystic name. By divulging her secret name, the demon becomes harmless and so departs.

In Jewish texts, it is always the prophet Elijah who appears instead of the saint or saints. The legend must already have been very ancient in this form, because – as has been mentioned before – it was known as far back as the fourth century B.C. to the Barbelo-Gnostics, who obviously must have taken it from Jewish sources.[1] Gradually, the tale was further embroidered and finally appeared as a 17th-century amulet text. The text involved is the one that was erroneously believed by *Montgomery*[2] to be from an Aramaic magic bowl from Nippur. It reads as follows:

> "Once, as the prophet Elijah was walking along, he met Lilith and her host. He said to her: O evil Lilith, whither do you go with your unclean host? And she replied: My Lord Elijah, I am about to go to the woman who has born a child to bring her the sleep of death, to take the child born to her away from her, to drink its blood, to suck the marrow from its bones and to leave its flesh over (alternative version: to gobble up its flesh). Elijah answered and said: I place you under the great ban, so that you may be turned into a speechless stone through the will of God. And Lilith said: My Lord, for God's sake, lift this spell so that I may fly away. I swear in the name of God that I will avoid the paths that lead to a woman with a newborn child. Whenever I hear or see my name, I will disappear at once. I will tell you my (secret) names. Whenever you pronounce these, neither I nor my host will have the power, to enter the house of a woman in childbirth and to torment her. I swear to you to reveal my names so that you may write them down and hang them in the room in which a newborn child lies... Whosoever knows these names, and writes them down, ensures that I will flee from the newborn child. Therefore, hang this amulet up in the room of a woman in childbirth."[3]

1. Cf. p. 104.
2. Cf. p. 104.
3. M. Gaster: *loc. cit.*, p. 1025. The legend cited by Montgomery differs from this version in several places

Afterwards, Lilith reveals all her secret names to the prophet. One of them is *Abizo,* which is probably connected with the terms Abyzou and Byza, which for their part are related to Obyzouth.[1] Another name for Lilith is *Ailo,* which has already made an appearance as Alû in the Babylonian invocation texts.[2]

To Lilith's earnest entreaty, Elijah replies:

"I conjure you and your host in the name of YHWH, the God of Israel, Abraham, Isaac and Jacob, in the name of the divine Shekhinah, in the name of the ten Seraphim, Ophanim and the divine beasts, may their names be praised, that you and your host do no harm to this woman..."

Then, Elijah employs a further invocation, taken from the ceremonial initiation formula:

"Sanvai. Sansanvai. Semangloph. Adam and Eve.
Out with Lilith."

It can be assumed from parallel legends that he frees Lilith from the ban and that she flies away.

There is a whole series of variations on this particular Elijah story, which have been collected by *Gaster,*[3] who was thus able to make a distinction between all their differing styles. As early as 1645, *Leo Allatius* published two Graeco-Byzantine versions.[4] As in all Byzantine texts, the child-stealing demon is called *Gello* or *Gyllo*[5] – Gilu in the corresponding Hebrew legends. This name also corresponds to the Babylonian Gallû. Gyllo is constantly seeking new-

1. Cf. p. 117
2. Cf. p. 38
3. M. Gaster: *loc. cit.,* p. 1005ff
4. M. Gaster: *loc. cit.,* p. 1018ff
5. Cf. p. 41

born Christian children, which she steals and kills. On her journey, she meets the two saints *Sisynios* and *Synodoros*. Gyllo has stolen the seven children of *Melitena*, the saints' sister. The two saints beat Gyllo until she begs for mercy:

> "Leave me, o saints of the Lord, and do not beat me any more. For I will tell you what may be done so that I am no longer able to enter the houses (of the Christians) and so that I stay 75 miles away from them… If a person writes down my twelve and a half names, I will not enter his house, neither the house of N., the servant of the Lord, nor that of his wife or his children, and I will stay 75 miles away… My first name is *Gyllo*, my second *Morrha*, my third *Byza*… and the half *Strigla*."[1]

Once the two saints have learned the secret names and Gyllo has returned Melitena's stolen children, they allow her to depart.

It is clear that Saints Sisynios and Synodoros correspond to the angels Sanvai and Sansanvai referred to in the Alphabet of ben Sira. Occasionally, a Saint Sisoe is named instead of these two saints in the Christian legend.

The Syrian invocation texts edited by *Gollancz*[2] refer to a "magic curse of Mar Abd'Isho, the monk and hermit of God." This saint, too, meets a female demon. He seizes her, binds her and curses her, in order to learn from her the secret of her hidden names. One of these names is Lilitha, another "strangling mother of young boys."[3]

A similar variant is told by *Pradel*. In this tale, which comes from present-day Greece but which is

---

1. M. Gaster: *loc. cit.,* p. 1021
2. H. Gollancz: *loc. cit.,* p. 69
3. H. Gollancz: *loc. cit.,* p. 84

based on far older, orally transmitted material, the archangel Michael coming down from Sinaï encounters the demonic *Abouzou*. He, too, asks her where she is going. She replies:

> "I creep into the houses like a snake, a reptile or a dragon. I bring all manner of evil. I cause the nursing mother's milk to dry up and wake children from their sleep to kill them."[1]

Reitzenstein[2] has published a legend which is similar to the above in every detail. The female demon in this version is called *Baskania, Baskosyne* or simply "the strangler," for short.

Gaster[3] has published a completely modern variant from the life of present-day Romanian farmers. The dangerous demon is called Avezuha, but has many other secret names, such as Avestitza. In this instance, the text has almost taken on the narrative attributes of a fairy tale – but its original mythical characteristics are, nonetheless, still clearly recognizable. *Umberto Cassuto* has edited a parallel text.

Also related to these legends is a tale of an Hispanic Jewess from Palestine, which was published by *Hanauer* and cited by *Thompson*[4] and later by *Joshua Trachtenberg*.[5] Here, too, a Lilith-like figure appears, whose name is *la brusha*. She forces her way into the maternity room in the form of a huge black cat and steals the child. The name is derived from the Span-

---

1. F. Pradel: *loc. cit.*, p. 23
2. R. Reitzenstein: *loc. cit.*, p. 297f
3. M. Gaster: *loc. cit.*, p. 1008f
4. R.C. Thompson: *Semitic Magic.* London, 1908, p. 42, note 1
5. J. Trachtenberg: *Jewish Magic and Superstition.* New York, 1939, p. 278, note 34

ish *bruja*[1] or the Portuguese *bruxa*, corresponding to
the Provençal *bruesche*. Like the Striges, the word
means a witch and a predatory night owl.

Commentary:

It must be extremely difficult, if not impossible, to
establish whether the Christian, i.e., the Graeco-Byzantine and the later Syrian, Ethiopian, South Slavonic and Romanian versions were created from Jewish
sources and only became christianized in some secondary phase. However, it cannot be ruled out that –
as *Gaster*[2] assumes – the Lilith legends originated in
the Middle East, perhaps in Babylonia. According to
this interpretation, they were then transmitted to the
Jews on the one hand, who Judaized them, and to the
Gnostic Manichaean sect on the other, and from that
– in a somewhat roundabout way – to the Neo-Man-
ichaean Bogomils in Bulgaria and to the Cathars and
Albigenses in the West.

The solution to this problem of priority is a matter
for the historico-religious researcher. Still, from the
psychological standpoint, one can also ask oneself
whether an archetypical motif might not be involved
which – independently of any direct influence
caused by migration – could appear in widely different times and places and which – depending on the
environment concerned – could assume either a
more Christian or a more Jewish bias.

In the Romanian texts published by *Gaster*, the
name of the demon is *Avestitza*. *Hugo A. Winkler*[3] has

1. L. Tolhausen: *Neues spanisch-deutsches und deutsch-spanisches
   Wörterbuch.* Leipzig, 1897, Vol. I, cf. bruja
2. M. Gaster: "Lilith und die drei Engel" in *Studies and Texts. loc. cit.,*
   p. 1257
3. H.A. Winkler: *loc. cit.*

assumed that this name is derived from the Slavonic Vjessica, i.e., witch. However, *Gaster*'s hypothesis, which links this term with the Obyzouth of the Testament of Solomon, strikes me as more obvious. Other, similar-sounding names for Lilith, like Abiza, Byza or Abouzou – which, according to *Schmidt*,[1] means bloodsucker – also point in this direction.

What all these legends have in common is the theme of a dangerous, female demon who is vanquished by one or two superior male saints or by a lone prophet, then rendered harmless and finally driven away. In this case, too, Lilith – or her equivalent demons – appears in her guise of a terrible mother. Except in a very few instances, the aspect of the seductive anima is totally absent. But it is typical that this side of her character is not directed against the saint – who is more a kind of tutelary spirit for the endangered mother and her children. In the *Melitena* version, the two saints stand up for their sister; in the *Avezuha* version, the archangel Michael is the guardian of Mary and the Christ child. In the *Abouzou* version, the archangel Michael again guards the endangered women and their children. It is typical that – apart from the reworking of the Jewish text by the Barbelo-Gnostics – it is always a male hero who vanquishes the demon. The woman is delivered up, defenseless, to the demon, without a fight. We will go into the psychological aspects of this motif at a later stage.

1. B. Schmidt: *loc. cit.*, p. 139ff

8) Lilith in Arabic Literature: the Karina

The Lilith myth found its expression in Arabic literature, too. The pertinent Arabic texts date from about the 13th century – by which time a Christian and Jewish tradition had already existed for centuries. In his book Schams al Ma'arif, the Arabic writer *al Buni,* whose main concern is with magic practices, refers to a child-stealing and child-killing demon, who appears under three different names. Frequently, she is called *Um-al-Sibjan,* i.e., Mother of Children,[1] and sometimes, *Tabi'a.* Mostly, however, she appears under the name *Karina.*

The original meaning of the word Karina is something like "female companion" and she corresponds to the male companion, or Karin, who is also mentioned. The Karina is a female demon and is still feared to this day in certain Arab countries, notably Egypt and Morocco.

In Arabic legends, as well, we find the familiar motif of the vanquishing of a female demon by a hero. Here, too, the demon is rendered harmless through the hero extracting from her the secret of her mystic name. In Arabic literature, this hero is generally King Solomon, the great lord and master over all spirits and demons, a motif which stems from Jewish sources.

According to one Arabic text, published by *Winkler:*

"Some sources report that he (Solomon) encountered the Karina one night. He found her dusky of countenance, and her eyes were deep blue in color. He asked

---

1. In the Zohar, too, Lilith is described as "mother of children" in one place. This description appears to have been borrowed from the Arabic

her: 'Whither do you go?' She replied: 'I go to the one who lies in his mother's womb, to eat his flesh, drink his blood and crush his bones.' Then he said: 'The curse of Allah be upon you, o accursed one.' And she said: 'Do not curse me, for I have twelve names. Whosoever knows them and hangs them round himself, him will I not go near. Whosoever writes them down has nothing to fear, by the will of Allah, the Almighty.'"[1]

Commentary:

Here, again, the Lilith-like figure appears as a child-stealing and child-killing demon. The blue color of her eyes refers to the belief common in the Mediterranean region and the East, that blue is the color of demons. The custom of painting many houses blue may possibly be associated with protection against demons.

What is completely new in the Arabic texts is the role of the Karina as a kind of shadow figure of the woman, just as on the other hand the Karin corresponds to the shadow of the man. Should the woman marry, then her Karina marries the man's Karin. Should the woman become pregnant, then the Karina launches into her devilish activities. First, she tries to drive the woman out and take her place. If the Karina meets the pregnant woman, she will strike her in the body to try to cause a miscarriage. If this does not succeed and the woman has children, the Karina will herself give birth to the same number of babies.

The Karina continually tries to create discord in the relations between husband and wife:

"I am the Karina. I make discord between man and wife. I cause the woman to have miscarriages. I make

1. H.A. Winkler: *loc. cit.,* p. 3

her infertile. I make men sterile. I fill married men with love for the wives of other men, married women with love for the husbands of other women. In short, I do the opposite of whatever makes married couples happy."[1]

Commentary:

In this text, the Karina has a further role, namely as a disrupter of marital relations. Lilith plays the same role in Jewish tradition. As a result, it cannot be established with any certainty whether *al Buni* knew of this motif, which is also to be found in the Zohar (written at about the same time), or whether – which is less likely – the author of the Zohar knew and made use of *al Buni's* work.

What is of psychological interest is the motif that Karin and Karina, the respective shadow figures, marry alongside husband and wife – thereby leading to a cross-cousin relationship between the four, which *Jung*[2] calls quaternio. It should be remembered, however, that this is not a classic marriage-quaternio in the sense employed by *Jung,* whereby husband and wife are united on the one hand and their respective animus and anima on the other. In our case, the result is the union of the two shadow figures, which gives the quaternio quite a different character.

Like Lilith, the Karina also appears to the husband in his erotic dreams and tries to seduce him and sleep with him. Like Lilith, again, she tries to steal the wife's child from its mother's womb and kill it.

1. H.A. Winkler: *loc. cit.,* p. 27
2. C.G. Jung: "Psychology of the Transference" in *The Practice of Psychotherapy.* Princeton & London, CW, 1954, Vol. XVI, p. 225

All over the Near East are numerous pictorial representations of the encounter between a saint, or a saintly hero, and a female demon. In these pictures, however, the emphasis is less on the attempt to extract the secret of her mystic name from the demon than on the demon's attempt to seduce the saint or hero – in other words, here the anima-character moves more into the foreground. It is in this guise that a 6th-century Coptic fresco depicts Saint Sisynios. The female demon is portrayed with her upper torso naked and her unbound hair streaming wildly behind her back. The woman tries to seduce the saint, but he resists her steadfastly. In other pictures, seductive women, completely or half-naked, with pronounced breasts and flowing hair, are shown being vanquished by Solomon or – in the Christian versions – by a saint.[1]

9) Lilith in the Kabbalah: Lilith and Samael

Prior to the later Middle Ages, the Lilith myth also found its way into the mystical Jewish writings known as the Kabbalah. Here, alongside her aspect of a child-stealing and child-killing female demon, Lilith clearly appears as a seductive woman, i.e., in her anima aspect.

The principal work of the Kabbalah, the Zohar, which was written at the beginning of the 14th century by the Spanish Kabbalist *Moses de León*, contains numerous passages in which Lilith is mentioned, either directly or indirectly. In these, the author borrows various motifs that appeared in earlier and part-

1. H.A. Winkler: *loc. cit.*, p. 163

ly non-Kabbalistic works, such as the Alphabet of ben Sira.[1]

In the Zohar, too, Lilith appears as the first wife of Adam, who left him after a bitter quarrel. Like the author of the Alphabet of ben Sira, the author of the Zohar also makes a link with the dual Creation story in Genesis. But, in addition, an old Talmudic tradition is continued in the Zohar.[2] In this version, the primordial man, Adam, originally had both male and female attributes. Only later was this hermaphrodite divided into two, with the side that was separated off becoming Eve:

> "The first man consisted of male and female elements, for it says (Gen. 1, 26): 'Let us make man in our image, after our likeness.' Thus he was made both male and female and was only divided later."[3]

To understand this passage, it must be explained that the Kabbalah makes a very precise distinction between the earthly first man (Adam rishon) and the heavenly, mythical, primordial man (Adam qadmon). The latter is an androgynous being and corresponds in part to the descriptions of primordial men in many different religions, e.g., to the Iranian Gayomard, the Indian Purusha, the Platonic primordial man and the Gnostic anthropos.

According to the Zohar, the subsequent creation of Eve through her separation from the similarly male/female first Adam is the essential reason for Lilith's departure:

> "Later God divided man into two and formed his female side. He brought her (Eve) to him like a bride to

1. Cf. p. 119
2. BT: Traktat Erubin 18a
3. Zohar II 55a

the bridal bed. When Lilith saw this, she fled and she still dwells in the towns of the sea coast, where she attempts to entrap men."[1]

Lilith is mentioned in several passages of the Zohar as the quintessential seductress of men, e.g., in the following extract:

"She (Lilith) adorns herself with all kinds of decorations, like an amorous woman. She stands at the entrance to roads and paths, in order to seduce men. She seizes the fool who approaches her, kisses him and fills him with a wine whose dregs contain snake venom. As soon as he has drunk this, he starts to follow her. When she sees that he has deserted the way of truth to follow, her, she takes off all that she originally put on for this fool. Her adornments for seducing men are her beautifully-dressed hair, red as a rose, her cheeks, white and red, her ears hung with chains from Egypt and her neck hung with all the jewels of the East. Her mouth is (tiny) like a narrow doorway, a graceful ornament, her tongue is sharp as a sword, her words soft as oil. Her lips are red as a rose, sweet with all the sweetness of the world. She is dressed in crimson, adorned with all the jewels in the world, with 39 pieces of jewelry. Those fools, who come to her and drink this wine, commit fornication with her. And what does she do then? She leaves the fool alone, sleeping in his bed, while she ascends into the heights (heaven). There, she gives a bad report of him. Then, she obtains permission to descend again. When the fool awakes, he assumes that he can take his pleasure with her, as before. She, however, removes her jewelry and turns into a powerful figure. She faces him, clothed in a fiery dress of flames. She arouses terror and causes body and soul to tremble. Her eyes are huge, in her hand is a sharp sword,

1. Zohar III 19a

from which bitter drops fall. She kills him (with this) and casts him into the very centre of hell."[1]

The text is of interest because it reveals Lilith's transformation after the successful seduction. At this point, the death-aspect of the terrible mother comes to the fore.

But, for the most part, Lilith is not concerned with killing men. She would rather seduce them, in order to conceive children by them:

"R. Isaac said: Since the time that Cain killed Abel, Adam was separated from his wife. At that time, two female spirits would come to him and have intercourse with him. He fathered demons and spirits by them, who roam the whole world. This is not surprising, because even today, if a man should dream while he sleeps, female figures frequently come to him and surround him. They conceive by him (through his nightly discharge) and then give birth. The creatures born in this fashion are called 'plagues of mankind'... In the same way, male spirits visit women and make them pregnant, so that they give birth to demons who are also called 'plagues of mankind.' "[2]

Besides Lilith, there are other female demonic beings who try to seduce men. Among them are *Machlat,* her daughter *Agrat* and, above all, *Na'amah* – who, in the Zohar, is virtually identified with Lilith. The Zohar says of Na'amah:

"Na'amah, however, conceives by them (men) in their lustful dreams. She becomes pregnant from this lust and gives birth to demons, who all go to the first Lilith, who raises them. She goes out into the world. When

1. Zohar I 148a/b
2. Zohar I 54b

she sees small children, she seizes them so as to kill them."[1]

In this text, a first Lilith, the companion of the demon prince Samael, is mentioned. In addition, the Zohar contains a second Lilith, wife of the demon prince Ashmedai. Referring to Na'amah, it goes on to say:

"Na'amah was the mother of demons and all those demons who sleep with men are descended from her."[2]

If such female spirits:

"... find men sleeping alone in a house, they surround them, and cling to them. Then they conceive by them. They also infect them with illnesses."[3]

The Kabbalistic tradition has added a new element to the Lilith myth: Lilith's relation with evil, which is personified as Satan or, as he is mostly called in the Zohar, *Samael.* In the post-Talmudic tradition, e.g., in the Pirqe de'Rabbi Eliezer, Samael is the leader of the fallen angels.

Scholem has established that the Lilith-Samael motif can be detected in earlier, pre-Zoharian literature. It is to be found in the writings of several Castilian Kabbalists – for example, the brothers *Isaac and Jacob ha'Cohen de Soria* and their pupil *Moses de Burgos,* all of whom probably took it from earlier, orally transmitted Oriental sources.[4]

---

1. Zohar I 19b & III 76b
2. Zohar I 56b
3. Zohar I 19b
4. G. Scholem: *Ursprung und Anfänge der Kabbala.* Berlin, 1962, p. 261f; G. Scholem: *Major Trends in Jewish Mysticism.* New York, 1961, p. 175

In the *Zohar,* Samael and Lilith – generally called "Samael and his companion" – are mentioned in numerous passages. They are portrayed as the proto-type of an "unholy pair" and thus, essentially, as the opponents of the "holy pair," i.e., the two Sefiroth, Tif'eret and Malchut. To understand these ideas, it is necessary to make a short digression into the Kabbalah – and particularly into the Kabbalah's teaching on the Sefiroth.[1]

The Jewish mystics' image of God – in complete contrast to the image painted by tradition and also to that of religious philosophers – is not a static one but one filled with an enormous inner dynamism.

From the remote, unknown and hidden source which the Kabbalists generally call en Sof – meaning something like the endless or unending being or thing – there developed the ten divine primordial numbers or Sefiroth, in a series of gradually unfolding emanations. En Sof is the indistinguishable being which rests on itself and is enclosed in itself, and which can only be described by conscious thought in negative or paradoxical phrases. And thus, it corresponds to the remote, unknown deus absconditus of the Christian mystics.

Then en Sof – through a spontaneous act of will – comes out of his state of peace and seclusion via an internal, divine process of evolution and develops into the Sefiroth, thus making himself available for the very first time to human meditation and knowledge. The sum total of the Sefiroth make up the Kabbalistic tree of life, whose roots are above and whose branches are below, or the Kabbalistic primordial man, Adam qadmon, who constitutes the heavenly prototype of earthly man, in that the individual Sefiroth correspond to human limbs or to a constantly turning wheel. The rich symbolism that the Kabbalists developed in conjunction with their teaching on the Sefiroth occupies a large area in the Judaico-mystic tradition.

The Sefiroth are mostly grouped in opposing pairs: thus there are right and left, male and female, active and passive Sefiroth. Within the Sefirothic system, however, two Sefiroth occupy a quite exceptional position. The very first two emanated Sefiroth, *Chochma* (Wisdom) and *Bina* (Understanding), are portrayed as a male and female pair of opposites, in which Chochma is the father and Bina the mother. However, this symbolism was applied in particular to the sixth Sefirah *Tif'eret* (Mercy) and the tenth Sefirah, which appears under different names. Sometimes it is referred to as *Malchut*, i.e., the Kingdom (of God), sometimes as *Shekhinah*, i.e., God's dwelling-place, and sometimes as *Kenesset Israel*, i.e., the community of Israel. But, in this case, it is not the earthly people of Israel that is meant but rather that people's heavenly prototype, just as Adam qadmon is the heavenly equivalent of the first man, Adam rishon. These ideas are based on the teaching on equivalence which is common to the Kabbalists, the alchemists and the philosophers: What is above is also below, or, in other words: The microcosm is nothing but a macrocosm, only in miniature and in reverse.

In the Sefiroth teaching, the Sefirah Tif'eret is the predominant male element of the divinity. On the opposite side to it is the Shekhinah, the female side of the divine personality, which is also occasionally personified. That God was recognized as having a female side is an almost revolutionary opinion of the

Kabbalah's which is completely alien to Biblical-Rabbinic Judaism, although this was acquainted with the idea of the Shekhinah. In this instance, however, the Shekhinah simply means God's presence in the world. Only in the Kabbalah did the decisive change occur that resulted in the feminine's inclusion in the divinity. It was supposed to represent a compensation for the devaluation of the feminine element in Judaism – but actually, through the inclusion of this feminine element in the divinity, a revaluation of the feminine was expressed.

The Shekhinah is frequently referred to as *Matronita,* i.e., mistress, or as *"supreme woman"* (isha eljona),[1] or – in accordance with other Gnostic ideas – as the *"light maiden,"*[2] in whose "secret, all that is female in the earthly world is founded."[3]

As long as unity and harmony existed within their world – the pleroma – all the Sefiroth were equally balanced, so that the divine stream of life flowed from en Sof through numerous connecting channels to the individual Sefiroth and animated and sustained them. At the same time, the two Sefiroth, Tif'eret and Shekhinah, form the centre of unity and totality in the divine pleroma. They are the divine or "holy pair," to which – on the earthly plane – corresponds the marriage between man and woman as conducted according to the sacraments.

One of the most complex problems of Jewish mysticism is the question of evil. Here, too, the Kabbalah reveals its Gnostic character, although it never leads

1. Zohar II 54b
2. Zohar III 180a
3. G. Scholem: "Schechina. Das weiblich-passive Moment in der Gottheit" in *Von der mystischen Gestalt der Gottheit.* Zurich, 1962, p. 177

to an antinomistic heterodoxy.[1] However, the question finds no simple, standardized answer in the Zohar. There is one version, according to which, evil originated from the independence and hypertrophy of the left, female Sefirah *Din,* i.e., the directing powers in God. According to this version of the Zohar, Samael and Lilith also originated from this side. Another opinion holds that the realm of the ten bright, pure Sefiroth is opposed by a correspondingly dark rival hierarchy of impure Sefiroth, the sum of which constitutes the so-called "other side" (sitra achra), or the "world of husks" (kelippot). This is the demonic, destructive side of the divine personality. It is in this dark sphere that the negative, demonic powers develop, which appear – personified – as Samael and Lilith. Hence, the "holy pair" is counterbalanced by an equally "unholy pair" of impure beings. And just as the "divine union," the hieros gamos, the union of the Divine King and the Shekhinah, guaranteed unity and harmony in God, the world and mankind, so within the sphere of impurity and evil the union of Samael and Lilith reflects the union of the female with evil.

Now, though, the primeval harmony of the world of the Sefiroth is disrupted. Through a tragic development that affects both God, the world and mankind, the divine stream of life is either cut off or diverted to the impure Sefiroth. The origin of this catastrophic development lies in the Fall of Adam, which is continued through the transgressions of each human individual. As a result, the original harmony is disrupted and chaos develops in the world of the Sefiroth: Nothing remains in the place in which

---

1. G. Scholem: "Gut und Böse in der Kabbala" in *loc. cit.,* p. 66ff

it belongs, everything is tossed about, jumbled up
and torn apart. And so the hieros gamos between
God and the Shekhinah is dislocated, thus strengthening the power of the "whorish woman,"[1] Lilith,
who attempts to take the place of the Shekhinah.[2]

The *unity* of God is expressed in the unity of His
name, the Tetragram YHWH. According to one version of the Zohar,[3] it is Lilith who tears apart the
unity of His divine name. According to Kabbalistic
belief, the Y (Yod) in this name corresponds to
Chochma, the first H (He) to Bina, the W (Wav) to
the Sefirah Tif'eret, while the second H (He) corresponds to the Shekhinah. In this connection, it says
of Lilith:

> "She it is who separates the two H's from each other
> and prevents the entry of the W between them. When
> Lilith stands between the one H and the other, then
> the Almighty, may His name be praised, cannot join
> them together."

As a result of this tragic development, the female
side is separated from the divine personality. Because God is cut off from His own female side, mind
and emotion – psychologically speaking – are no
longer united in an harmonious fashion.

The Shekhinah, who has lost her place beside
God, now goes into *exile* with the Jewish people.
Thus, on the divine plane, this event reflects the
Shekhinah's homelessness, and, on the human
plane, the expulsion of the people from their land.
Different opinions exist in the Zohar as to whether

1. Zohar I 148b
2. Zohar III 69a
3. Zohar I 27b

the Shekhinah's exile is voluntary or whether she was forced by God to go into exile with the people.

But one day, when the Messiah – and, with him, redemption – comes, the Jewish people will return to their land, and with them, the Shekhinah, who will then resume her rightful place. The original harmony will be recreated and "God and His name [shall be] one."[1]

One of the most profound and glorious concepts of the Kabbalah is reflected in this view, according to which, man – who yearns for redemption – not only needs God, but, vice versa, God also needs man, so that the state of harmony and unity may be recreated. Thus, man becomes the redeemer of God, in that through his behavior, through prayer, repentance and meditation, he hastens the Shekhinah's return to God.

In the description, filled with high dramatic tension, of his death, R. Simon ben Jochai – who was for centuries believed to be the author of the Zohar – reveals with visionary force the new hieros gamos between the Divine King and His Shekhinah.

10) Amulets against Lilith

That the Lilith myth, and above all, the fear of this demonic figure, has remained vividly alive to the present day is testified to by the vast number of amulets which have been preserved since the tenth century and which are still being manufactured today. Originally, the amulets consisted of handwritten texts on parchment – with the occasional printed text appearing on paper from the beginning of the

1. Zech. 14, 9

18th century. Frequently, engraved metal tablets were employed, which were hung up in the maternity room or round the necks of the mother and child. To these belong the so-called *Kimpet* papers, i.e., childbed papers, which were pinned to the four walls of the maternity room.

T. Schrire[1] has published a large number of such amulets from numerous eras and countries, such as Germany, Persia, Afghanistan, Morocco, Kurdistan and Palestine. The shape of the amulet varies a great deal. Generally, the tablets are square, but occasionally they are oval. Now and then, they are similar to mandalas. On other occasions, they are shaped like a Star of David, whose seven fields contain inscriptions, or a hand which – like the Arab peoples' Hand of Fatima – is supposed to afford protection. On a silver amulet from Irbid, on Lake Genazareth, is inscribed:

> "In the name of the great God, Amen. Hallelujah, for ever, Amen. Peace for Marian, daughter of S., and the unborn child in her womb, from the Lilith of her bridal bed."[2]

Reference has already been made to the best-known amulet text, which describes the encounter between Lilith and the prophet Elijah.[3]

On the amulets, Lilith is either invoked and conjured by her real name – as in the example above – or by her secret names, like Alû and Gilû. Many

---

1. T. Schrire: *Hebrew Amulets. Their Decipherment and Interpretation.* London, 1966, p. 149ff
2. J.A. Montgomery: "Some early Amulets from Palestine" in JAOS, New Haven, 1911, Vol. XXXI, p. 272ff
3. Cf. p. 130

amulets carry pictorial representations of Lilith in chains.

The larger amulets contain texts with invocations to the three angels who made an agreement with Lilith, or to Adam and Eve and the patriarchs and matriarchs. And they never fail to contain the command: Out with Lilith.[1]

Now and again, instructions are also given to draw a magic chalk circle round the bed of a woman who has just given birth.[2] According to *Isidor Scheftelowitz*, it is customary among Slavonic Jews to

> "make circles of coal or sodium bicarbonate on the walls of the room to protect a woman who has just given birth from evil spirits, and outside these circles to write the words: Adam, Eve, out with Lilith. And on the doors of the room, to write the names: Sanvai, Sansan-vai and Semangloph. Among medieval Jews, after the birth of a boy, the father would take great care during the first eight days to close the doors every evening, and would spend many hours reading from the Bible in the presence of those close relatives who had gathered in the new mother's room. Then he would draw a circle with the point of his sword around the bed in which lay the mother and child."[3]

Such apotropaic practices were, however, not at all confined to Slavonic Jews. About 1472, *Elias Levita* – whom *Israele Zoller* quotes – refers to the Alphabet of ben Sira and says à propos of the Ashkenazim, i.e., the Jews of German and Eastern European origin:

> "It was the custom to draw a circle of vitriol or coal on the wall of the room of a woman who had just given

1. L. Blau: *Das altjüdische Zauberwesen*. Budapest, 1898, p. 86ff
2. J. Trachtenberg: *loc. cit.*, p. 169
3. I. Scheftelowitz: *Die altpersische Religion und das Judentum*. Giessen, 1920, p. 77f

birth. In this was written: Adam and Eve. Out with Lilith."[1]

Zoller comments on this custom as follows:

"In Venice, and possibly in many other Jewish communities in Italy, the belief in Lilith has fallen completely into oblivion. But in numerous small towns in Poland, Russia and the Orient, Lilith doesn't represent a belief, she is a reality with which one must reckon when a birth is imminent and during the first week thereafter."[2]

Commentary:

Amulets, magic protective circles and prayers over the new mother were in common practice in former times. True, it seems as if they have become less frequent nowadays. But I was repeatedly assured in Israel that such amulets were in widespread use among primitive Jewish families, particularly those from Arab countries like Morocco and Tunisia, and also in Iran. They confirm *Zoller*'s conclusion that, even today, for many Jews, Lilith is a reality towards whom a cautious attitude is demanded. Such a magical viewpoint is no longer adequate for most people. However, a psychological attitude can give us an understanding of the reality and effect of Lilith as an inner figure.

1. I. Zoller: "Lilith" in RdA, Rome, 1926, p. 374
2. My own translation from the Italian

Part II

Psychological Section:

On the Psychology of the Lilith Myth

1) The First Encounter: The Lilith Dream

After the preceding historical and mythological investigations, the obvious questions are: What is the relevance of this myth today? Where is what present-day theologians tend to call its "place in life"? Or, in other words, is this myth still alive and what does it have to say to modern man?

Just how alive it *has* remained is evident from the numerous amulets we have mentioned. However, it is also of relevance in the individual sphere, as is shown in a dream picture of a contemporary man – an extremely depressive Jewish analysand, about 40 years old, who had a predominantly intellectual and intuitive nature. Some two years after the start of his analysis, which was chiefly concerned with the problem of shadow, he saw the following dream picture:

> "It is night, and I am lying in my bed, awake but with my eyes closed. All of a sudden, a beautiful female figure floats in through the closed window and comes to a halt to the left of my bed. She looks at me with a grave face, but speaks not a word. The upper half of her body is naked, her breasts are very prominent. Her skin is deep black in color. She has huge dark eyes and her black hair streams in a wild and unbound mass down her back. From her back sprouts a pair of wings. I find the woman highly attractive and seductive. I am fascinated by her, but at the same time I am afraid of her and do not dare to speak to her."

Associations:

On waking, the dreamer spontaneously associated two ideas. The first association runs as follows:

"I am black, but comely." The second:
"This is the harlot, Lilith."

Interestingly enough, these associations lack any reference to Lilith as Adam's first wife, whom the dreamer must have known from the Walpurgis Night scene in *Goethe's* Faust.

Commentary:

The first quotation that occurred to the dreamer is taken from the *Song of Songs*,[1] while the second association, which underlines the harlot character of this figure, refers to a side of Lilith's nature that is emphasized time and again in mythology and religious history.

It is probably no coincidence that a quotation from the *Song of Songs* (which was, incidentally, well-known to him) occurred to the dreamer.

According to the views of contemporary critical biblical science, which began with *J.G. Herder,* the *Song of Songs* is a collection of ancient Oriental love songs of an erotic, even sensual character. These songs were recited at every marriage celebration, during which the bride and groom were fêted as queen and king. According to *W. Wittekind,*[2] these love songs were originally based on archaic ritual songs from the Tammuz-Ishtar cult.

In the *Song of Songs,* an exchange of songs between a shepherd and a shepherdess takes place. The shepherd is also described as King Solomon, which gives rise to the assumption that Solomon himself may be the author of the text. The beloved is called the

1. *Song of Songs* 1, 5. The Zurich Bible translates the Hebrew word shachor, i.e., black, erroneously by brown
2. W. Wittekind: *Das Hohe Lied und seine Beziehungen zum Ischtarkult.* Hanover, 1925, p. 180ff

Shulamite, a name whose meaning has not yet been convincingly clarified. In early times, already, a tendency was gaining acceptance in both Jewish and Christian biblical exegesis, which attempted to give the *Song of Songs* a new, allegorical meaning. In the Jewish allegories, it was applied to YHWH and Israel, in the Christian variants to Christ and the Ecclesia, and since *Bernard de Clairvaux* to Christ and the soul. This change of meaning may possibly have been the reason why the book was admitted into the canon of holy writings at the Council of Jabne (circa 100 A.D.), despite numerous objections. However, that the original meaning was capable of preservation by later, Jewish biblical commentators is evident, for example, in *Samuel ben Me'ir,* who draws on parallel songs of the old French troubadours as explanation, and also in *Abraham ibn Ezra,* who cites Arabian love songs in comparison.

In the *Song of Songs,* the Shulamite says of herself:

"I am black, but comely, as the tents of Kedar, as the curtains of the Salmaers. Look not upon me, because I am black, because the sun hath looked upon me."

Clearly, the Kedarenes and Salmaers were nomads, who, like the Arabian nomads of today, lived in black tents.

In our Lilith dream, the dream figure represents the unconscious, female side of the dreamer, i.e., personifying what *Jungian psychology* usually calls the anima. It emerges clearly from the entire context that, in this case, a figure from the dreamer's conscious world is not involved. If we attempt to reduce such an apparition to the dreamer's own mother or to the figure of a girl from his external reality, then, as *Jung* stresses,

"… the real meaning of the figure naturally gets lost in the process, as is inevitably the case with all these reductive interpretations whether in the sphere of the psychology of the unconscious or of mythology. The innumerable attempts that have been made in the sphere of mythology to interpret gods and heroes in a solar, lunar, astral or meteorological sense contribute nothing of importance to the understanding of them; on the contrary, they all put us on a false track."[1]

From numerous parallels which have been consulted, it emerges plainly that a suprapersonal, archetypal figure is involved here. The two associations also point to a dual aspect of the figure: on the one hand, the anima image appears personified as the majestic beloved of the king, and on the other as a seductive harlot.

Contrasts are specific for all archetypal figures, especially when they stand on the threshold of the conscious. In the course of the progressive process of the dawning of consciousness, the inherent opposites draw apart, with the result that they can be distinguished by the conscious, which always thinks and perceives in opposites.

In this dream, Lilith appears exclusively in her anima role, and all the other aspects that she possesses in myth, legend and folklore fade into the background – which may well arise from the fact that the dreamer is a man. Were Lilith to appear in a woman's dream, it must be assumed that quite different sides of her character would come to the fore.

The *bright* image of the anima is embodied in the Shulamite, the *dark* one in the harlot Lilith. Howev-

1. C.G. Jung: "The Psychological Aspects of the Kore" in *The Archetype and the Collective Unconscious.* Princeton & London, 1959, CW, Vol. IX, p. 199

er, the former is described in only the vaguest of terms, while, conversely, the features of the "harlot Lilith" are very clearly detailed. The fact that, in the dream, the dark aspect predominates may perhaps be an indication that an over-clear anima image exists in the dreamer's conscious. The appearance of such a dark and frightening dream figure would, in this case, signify a correction of the dreamer's conscious attitude, since experience shows that the unconscious tends to compensate for one-sided conscious behavior. Thus – to take just one example – it is known from the psychology of neuroses that an extremely bright mother image often exists in the conscious, while in the unconscious the image of a terrible, devouring mother predominates. If, on the other hand, a markedly dark mother image dominates in the conscious, then it is to be assumed that, in the unconscious, a bright, kindly, caring, nurturing, mother figure will appear.

The *atmosphere* of the dream is neither particularly gloomy nor cheerful, but it is obviously very serious. However, there is something remarkably unreal attached to it: the dreamer has his eyes closed, and yet he can still see the dream figure. The window is closed, and yet the figure still manages to float into the room.

Lilith's apparition was an absolutely numinous experience for the dreamer. At first, he didn't ask himself what it meant. But his emotions were deeply stirred by it and he made repeated attempts to paint it. The painted picture corresponded to a great extent to the dream picture. Only after a few months did he become aware of his ambivalent emotional reactions. It became evident to him that what was involved had to be an experience from his own inner depths.

The ambivalence of the dreamer's feelings was apparent from his alternating between an intense fascination and an equally violent fear, with the latter finally prevailing. It was possibly also the principal reason why he didn't dare to talk to his dream figure. Perhaps the experience was also so overpowering that he couldn't talk and so was content to watch and observe the dream image.

And incidentally, he remained completely passive. Such a passive attitude on the part of the dreamer is highly unsatisfactory from the psychological point of view. Because he fails to act or react in the course of the event, he is not involved in it enough from an internal standpoint. One has to ask oneself what the attitude of the dreamer would have been if this figure had approached him in real life. In all probability, he would not merely have observed her and walked past her; it is more likely that he would have attempted to start up a conversation with her.

Jung[1] described a very similar dream experience, in which a dreamer looks on in complete indifference while his fiancée runs out onto a sheet of ice and slowly sinks into a fissure, without his rushing to help her. In our dream, there is no danger for the dreamer's anima. But his passivity is still alarming, because it is the expression of his distorted relationship with the unconscious. It is true that the encounter with the archetypal image denoted an intense fascination, as frequently occurs in the case of such internal pictures. But, at the same time, equally in-

1. C.G. Jung: "The Relations between the Ego and the Unconscious" in *Two Essays on Analytical Psychology*. Princeton & London, 1953, CW, Vol. VII, p. 213ff

tense fears arose of somehow falling under this image's spell. These fears increased at times to such an extent that the dreamer was afraid he might be undergoing a psychosis. In the course of the analysis, though, he gradually acquired inner strength and, parallel with this, underwent a change in his passive attitude towards the unconscious. This became evident from the fact that, slowly, an inner dialogue with the dream image began. The end of this developmental phase was constituted by an active imagination that occurred some five years later, in which Lilith appeared once again as a totally different figure.

However, first of all, we should consider the dream picture in greater detail. The *position* of Lilith on the left of the dreamer has a double significance. Firstly, it points to the fact that this figure remains to a large extent in the dreamer's unconscious. The *left* side generally represents the unconscious in both mythology and the dream interpretation of analytical psychology, while the right side symbolizes the conscious. Now, the left side – from the standpoint of critical conscious judgment – generally has a dark, frightening, even ill-omened nature. This is indicated by the double meaning of the Latin word sinister, which means left as well as ill-omened. As a result of her position on the left of the dreamer, the dangerous, frightening aspect of Lilith is also underlined. The *black color* of the dream figure relates her to other black goddesses, such as Isis, Parvati, Artemis and the various black statues of the Virgin in Einsiedeln, Czestochowa, Guadalupe and elsewhere. This black color, too, has a double significance. On the one hand, it points to the dreamer's unconsciousness in relation to this dream content; on the other, it underlines once again the dark character. The black of the prima materia of the alchemists is an expression of their unconsciousness. In addition, it is a dangerous state which must first of all be "washed" in the course of a lengthy transformation process, to bring out the different colors of albedo, citrinitas and rubedo, which signify a stimulation of the unconscious. At the same time, the dangerous nigredo is eliminated.

The *black hair,* which streams wild and unbound down Lilith's back, and her huge black eyes are the expression of unrestrained natural and physical desires. But the nakedness of the upper part of the body has another significance – probably involving a more sacral form of symbolism. In the Mycenean cult, exposing the breasts is a part of the sacral rites of the Cretan priestesses. The same displaying of breasts occurs in the Near Eastern cultural area, for example in the case of the goddesses of Ras Shamra[1] or the numerous Astarte figures with naked upper parts. They all point to a connection between these figures and the archetypal figure of the Great Mother.

The dreamer was particularly impressed by Lilith's two wings. When he saw them, he was reminded of his initiation dream, which he experienced when he was about four years old and which accompanied him throughout his whole life:

> "I have two huge wings and use them to fly around the room. I can also fly through closed doors. I use them to fly from the first floor down through the stairwell to the cellar, where I'm supposed to be looking for some-

---

1. E. Neumann: *loc. cit.,* pl. 123

thing. I am highly fascinated by this task, but I'm also afraid of the dark cellar."

Lilith's two wings in the dream picture are a sign that, clearly, what is involved is not a being from the dreamer's conscious world. Lilith is a figure from the world beyond, the world of myths, dreams, of the unconscious.

The wings, too, are an indication of descent from the Great Mother, as the numerous portrayals of winged mother goddesses show. Thus, for example, in Egypt, the winged Isis is a protective, defensive goddess. As a corpse-eating vulture, she is the mistress of death.

To sum up, we can say that the appearance of the anima in its dual aspect is heralded in this dream picture, in which the dark side of the dream figure predominates.

2) Lilith and Saturn: Melancholy

At the beginning of this section, I mentioned that our dreamer was of a particularly melancholic disposition. In the following pages, therefore, we will be considering whether this melancholy might be linked with the appearance of the Lilith picture – and, if so, in what way.

The dreamer's *melancholy* was a distressing experience for him. It was not continually present, but at certain times it intensified to such a degree that it led to lengthy periods of depression that not only undermined his self-confidence but also led to destructive self-criticism. Indeed, it reached the point of threatening to destroy his willingness to work and even his will to live.

Depressive states, as psychopathology shows, may occur in association with a wide variety of psychic disorders. Such disruptive factors may be of a purely *exogenous* nature. Among these belong, for example, chronic intoxications and states of physical exhaustion. With more *endogenously* conditioned disorders, e.g., the manic-depressive syndrome, symptoms are involved whose origins are for the most part difficult to comprehend. How far influences of heredity or environment are relevant in such cases is a controversial question.

In addition, there are psychogenic disorders which can also be connected with depressive states. Among these belong the so-called *relief depressions*. Neurotic states are a specific kind of psychogenic depression and may, again, be based on the most varied causes. Not infrequently, unconscious fears, unresolved sexual conflicts and unconscious aggressions are responsible for them.

However, the various kinds of depression cannot always be clearly delimited one from the other, as the borders between them are highly fluid.

And again, there are certain depressive states which can be explained by a particular, possibly genetically conditioned nature, in which neither an exogenous nor an endogenous component can be clearly detected. These involve depressions which are connected in some not yet completely understood fashion with creative processes. For this kind of depression, I would favor the term "creative melancholy." A neurotic component may be involved but its presence is not obligatory. Such depressions occur frequently before the start of, but occasionally also during, a creative phase, whereas depressions after the end of such a phase generally belong to the class of relief depressions.

Such states can be easily detected in creative people, especially in visual artists, musicians, poets and philosophers.

If one investigates such depressions, one often comes across the so-called *Saturnine nature* of a creative person. This leads us to investigate the link between Saturn and melancholy and, as a result, to the question of the connection between Lilith and Saturn.

In antiquity, the Roman god Saturn, who corresponds to the Greek Kronos, was already identified with a planet, which thus also received the name of Saturn.

The god Saturn is an ambivalent figure: on the one hand, he is the dispenser of wisdom, maturity, constancy, intelligence and creative powers. The positive sides appear in the foreground in medieval *philosophy* in particular, especially in Neo-Platonism. On the other hand, in medieval, Occidental *astrology*, a completely opposing interpretation asserted itself. Here, Saturn is without exception a maleficus, an unlucky star – not only responsible for all sorts of illness, crime and death, but also throwing men into gloom, extreme loneliness, melancholy and despair. Not for nothing can the Spanish words saturnino and the English saturnine mean either "Saturnian" or "melancholic." This inspires a short digression into the teachings of antiquity and the Middle Ages on the four temperaments, particularly melancholy.

The temperaments, or "complexities," which were already known in early antiquity, were based on the correct mixture and temperature of the four basic fluids or humors. This "humoral teaching," whose origins go back to *Hippocrates,* was later developed further and recorded in writing by *Celsus, Soranus, Aretaeus* and others,[1] as well as by Arabic astrologers of the 9th and 10th centuries. According to the so-called correspondence teaching, which was common throughout the whole of antiquity and also partly during the Middle Ages, the below corresponded to an above, the microcosm to the macrocosm and vice versa.

Accordingly, the four *planetary gods,* Jupiter, Mars, Saturn and Mercury, were assigned *bodily fluids* or biles corresponding to the nature of these planets, as well as the *organs* in which the humors are produced. This is illustrated in the following division of types:

Jupiter: warm and damp – green bile – liver – sanguine
Mars: warm and dry – yellow bile – liver – choleric
Saturn: cold and dry – black bile – spleen – melancholic
Mercury: cold and damp – white bile – lungs – phlegmatic

If one pursues the evaluation of these four temperaments, it becomes apparent that in Greece, above all, the "jovial," sanguine temperament is the ideal, while the others, especially the melancholy temperament, are described as morbid behavior. According to *Galen,* melancholy has its seat in the hypochondrium, i.e., the part of the body beneath the breastbone and the ribs. In this connection, he speaks of morbus hypochondriacus.

A change in these views, however, is already apparent in *Aristotle,* the younger contemporary of Hippo-

---

1. E. Fischer-Homberger: *Hypochondrie.* Bern, Stuttgart & Wien, 1970, p. 14ff

crates. As Saturn was originally a highly ambiguous figure, so in *Aristotle* is melancholy also ambivalent, in that he distinguishes between a morbid melancholy (melancholia dia noson) and a natural melancholy (melancholia dia physin). Because, according to him, the black bile of the spleen (mélaina cholè) may – in the right dose and at the right temperature – help men to great intellectual achievements, while on the other hand severe depressions can arise from the wrong dosage and overheating.

These ideas were taken further during the Renaissance, above all in the Florence of the Medici by *Dante* and *Petrarch,* but especially by the doctor and humanist *Marsilio Ficino.* Like *Petrarch, Ficino* was subject to acute melancholy. In his exchange of letters with Giovanni Cavalcanti,[1] he mentions that he himself has suffered "the bitterness of melancholy and the malignance of Saturn" in his own body. Yet he also recognizes that it was the selfsame Saturn that spurred him to intellectual and creative activity. This was presumably also the reason that made it possible for him to accept his melancholy, which is why he describes Saturn as the "noblest and mightiest star"[2] and melancholy as a "unique and divine gift."[3]

The view, already widespread in antiquity, that three activities – imaginatio, ratio and mens – exist within the soul was adopted later by *Agrippa von Nettesheim.*[4] According to Agrippa, all three activities of the soul or mind fall under the rule of Saturn and

---

1. E. Panofsky & F. Saxl: "Dürers Melencolia I" in *Studien der Bibliothek Warburg.* Leipzig & Berlin, 1923, Vol. II, p. 33
2. E. Panofsky & F. Saxl: *loc. cit.,* p. 35
3. E. Panofsky & F. Saxl: *loc. cit.,* p. 34
4. F. Nordström: *Goya, Saturn and Melancholy.* Uppsala, 1962, p. 131

his "furor melancholicus." *Johann Caspar Lavater*[1] goes still further, saying of the mind:

> "And so, at the same time, it is in the habit of also drawing to itself another, even more noticeable and less changeable characteristic, namely a solemn, gentle and profound melancholy. This state of mind is truly the inseparable companion of genius."

The connection between saturnine nature, melancholy and intellectual, artistic creativity may easily be demonstrated by a few examples.

Every important intellectual or artistic work is, when all is said and done, a statement about the person who created it. It was *Leonardo da Vinci* who coined the phrase: "Every painter paints himself," and *Albrecht Dürer* stressed in similar vein that: "Many painters produce something that resembles them." Indeed, *Dürer* is a particularly striking example of the connection between saturnine melancholy and creative talent. This finds expression above all in Melencolia I, one of his three famous engravings on the subject. The picture shows a winged female figure with an earnest expression. As in the Lilith dream, here, too, the wings indicate that this is not a figure from the artist's conscious world but one which comes from the unconscious. She sits in deepest self-absorption, surrendered to her fate. A winged animal – possibly a bat – bears on one wing the inscription: Melencolia I. On the floor lies a sleeping dog; in the center of the picture is a child – also winged – whose significance is not completely clear.[2] Besides

---

1. F. Nordström: *loc. cit.*, p. 131
2. G.R. Heyer: *Dürers Melancholie und ihre Symbolik*. Zurich, 1935, p. 231ff is contestable on many points, both iconographically and psychologically

all kinds of allegorical objects such as a bell, an hourglass and scales, lie various tools which correspond to the occupations that come under Saturn. The enema syringe, the garland of damp leaves that the woman wears on her head, as well as the magic counting quadrate, symbolize the means by which man attempted to master melancholy in those days. The picture, as *E. Panofsky* and *F. Saxl* emphasize, is "nothing more than an intellectual self-portrait of *Albrecht Dürer*," who originally planned engravings of all four temperaments but who

> "did not depict (the other three), because he could not identify himself with them."[1]

That *Dürer* himself had to combat deep melancholy is also clear from a remark made by his younger contemporary *Melanchthon*, who speaks of the "melancholia generosissima Duereri." As a result, both Dürer experts call Melencolia I a true confession of the artist. It reflects

> "... the face of the aged Saturn, which gazes at us; we alone have the right to distinguish Dürer's features in it, too."[2]

Depressive features show up even more clearly in the artistic work of *Francisco de Goya. Goya* was an artist of genius who, besides going through extremely euphoric phases, was overcome time and again by utmost dejection and the blackest of moods, which cannot be explained solely by his constantly varying external fate. This may be seen from one of his early cartoons, Cita, and in the pen-and-ink drawing of the woman in front of the mirror in the cycle, The Four

1. E. Panofsky & F. Saxl: *loc. cit.*, p. 74
2. E. Panofsky & F. Saxl: *loc. cit.*, p. 76

Temperaments. *Goya*'s melancholy shows clearly in the sketches for print 43 of the Caprichos. The title of one sketch, made in 1797, reads: "The sleep of reason begets monsters." It depicts a sleeping man, surrounded by animals of the night, such as a lynx, and by bats. These are animals that belong to the darkness, which are under the control of Saturn and symbolize his melancholy. In the third sketch, the aquatint version, an owl hands the painter a brush. That the author himself is represented in this case is clear from the second version, in which the sleeper is referred to as "el autor soñando." The picture not only shows *Goya*'s profound melancholy, but also his artistic genius. *F. Nordström*[1] points out that, here, *Goya*:

> "... has displayed himself as overwhelmed by disastrous melancholy but at the same time also as an artist and genius."

The fits of severe depression that afflicted *Goya* towards the end of his life show up most starkly in the *pinturas negras* from the Quinta de San Isidoro, above all in the gruesome Saturn picture.[2]

Melancholic fits and their intensification into truly depressive phases frequently find expression in artistic works. Indeed, it appears that especially gifted people can make creative use of their depressiveness. This is equally true for musicians, poets and visual artists. *Dürer* and *Goya* have already been advanced as examples of the latter. In literature, particularly impressive examples are to be found in the lyric works

1. F. Nordström: *loc. cit.*, p. 222
2. E. Lafuente-Ferrara & A. Pérez-Sánchez have pointed out that, on the basis of X-ray examinations, the pictures were originally less black, but Goya subsequently painted over them

of *Giacomo Leopardi* (the poem: Le ricordanze) and above all in the "poète saturnien" *Paul Verlaine* (the poem: Chanson d'Automne). In music, too, there are examples enough, such as *W.A. Mozart* (String quintet in G minor, K516) or *G. Mahler* (Tragic Symphony Nr. 6 in A minor). In modern philosophy, we should mention *Søren Kierkegaard*, who is a striking example of how a man can draw creative powers from deep depression.

Even the *alchemist* experiences a great variety of depressions, particularly at the beginning and during the course of the transformation process. He usually describes this condition as hell, chaos, blackness or darkness. Numerous alchemists, such as *Michael Maier, Gerhardus Dorneus* and the anonymous author of the book Rabbi Eleazar's Ancient Chemical Work – who is, presumably, a Christian alchemist, despite a great number of Hebraisms, and is known as *Pseudo-Eleazar* – speak of the initial tenebrositas or nigredo, which are also occasionally clearly referred to as melancholia. From them there later developed the green lion, the representative of an unbridled life threat, which, at the end of the day, was aimed at the entirety.[1]

Even the Shulamite, who was vaguely mentioned in our dream picture, appears in alchemy, in which she is a widely-used symbol. Here, it is not Lilith who is black but the Shulamite. *Pseudo-Eleazar* says that her initial black color must be washed off so that she can be "illuminated." In similar fashion, the external black of the lead, which is known to correspond to Saturn, must be removed so that the "inner gold" can

---

1. C.G. Jung: *Psychologische Interpretation von Kinderträumen und älterer Literatur über Träume.* Zurich, 1938/39, p. 170ff

appear. In this way, the dark, cold planetary god can be changed, so as to become the lord of wisdom and constancy.

With these remarks, we have touched on somewhat remote areas which appear to have little connection with our problem.

Yet it is now that we can actually verify a close connection between Lilith on the one hand and Saturn and melancholy on the other, on the basis of a particular passage from the Zohar. The teaching of *Hippocrates* is completely familiar to the Zohar, too. It says of Lilith:

> "The black bile from the spleen (corresponds to) Lilith. She (is under the) control of Saturn. She is the melancholy of the nethermost kingdom of the dead, of poverty, darkness, weeping, lamentation and hunger."[1]

Melancholic people who are under the control of Lilith – and, through her, of Saturn – are clearly designated as "Sons of Lilith" in the Zohar.

On the basis of the above passage, it seems almost impossible to me that the melancholic state of our dreamer and the appearance of the Lilith picture from his unconscious could be merely coincidental. But what kind of connection there is between them is difficult to determine. For example, it is conceivable that the appearance of Lilith is a direct reflection of the dreamer's melancholy. However, the exact reverse could also be possible, with the state of melancholy being activated or constellated by the appearance of the Lilith image.

It is equally difficult to state with any certainty whether the appearance of the archetypal image can

1. Zohar III 227b

be explained away by heredity. *Jungian* psychology makes a clear distinction between the "archetype in itself" and the "archetypal image." According to *Jung*, the former is:

> "an irrepresentable factor, a disposition which starts functioning at a given moment in the development of the human mind and arranges the material of consciousness into definite patterns."[1]

According to *Jung*, the individual archetypes:

> "exist preconsciously and presumably they form the structural dominants of the psyche in general. They may be compared to the invisible presence of the crystal lattice in a saturated solution."[2]

And thus, according to *Jung*, archetypes are also:

> "eternally inherited forms and ideas which have at first no specific content. Their specific content only appears in the course of the individual's life, when personal experience is taken up in precisely these forms."[3]

Consequently, whereas the archetypal structure of the psyche – that is to say, the archetype in itself – is directly inherited, the same is not necessarily true of archetypal pictures and ideas, in which the archetype per se compresses itself. *Jung* expressed himself in contradictory fashion in this connection. On the one hand, he says that inheritance of archetypal pictures

1. C.G. Jung: "A Psychological Approach to the Dogma of the Trinity" in *Psychology and Religion: West and East*. Princeton & London, 1958, CW, Vol. XI, p. 148f
2. C.G. Jung: *loc. cit.*, p. 149, note 2
3. C.G. Jung: "Psychological Commentary on *The Tibetan Book of the Dead*" in *loc. cit.*, p. 518

is "difficult if not impossible to prove,"[1] but on the other hand, he admits:

> "I must confess that I have never yet found infallible evidence for the inheritance of memory images, but I do not regard it as positively precluded that in addition to these collective deposits which contain nothing specifically individual, there may also be inherited memories that are individually determined."[2]

The above-mentioned dream might indicate that an inheritance of archetypal pictures could be within the bounds of possibility – for the dream picture corresponds to the picture of Lilith as it is known from Jewish tradition. Thus, the Zohar usually calls Lilith the "black one, the false one or the harlot."[3]

Let us return again to our point of departure. At first, the dreamer was neither intuitively nor intellectually aware of the background to his states of depression. He found his condition agonizing and felt himself to be at the mercy of superior forces which he was powerless to resist. But any intellectual understanding of his situation would have been of little help to him.

To conclude this section, let us briefly examine how depth psychology views the problem of melancholy.

In his work on grief and melancholy, *Freud*[4] elaborated a difference between the two states. According to him, grief is conditioned by the real, i.e., external

1. C.G. Jung: *loc. cit.*, p. 103
2. C.G. Jung: "The Relations between the Ego and the Unconscious" in *Two Essays on Analytical Psychology*. Princeton & London, 1953, CW, Vol. VII, p. 190
3. Zohar I 148b
4. S. Freud: *Mourning and Melancholia*. London, 1957, Standard Edition, Vol. 14, p. 428

loss of a love object, either through death or by the object turning away from the Ego. Under normal circumstances, the "respect of reality" will gradually assert itself in such a case and the Ego will be restored to its former condition "at the end of the period of mourning," i.e., it will once again be free and untrammeled.

Freud holds that the situation is somewhat different in the case of melancholy. As with grief, a "bond between the libido and a particular person" was originally forged. However, as a result of a "real affront or disappointment" on the part of the love object, this object relationship is severely shaken. This is made all the more possible either because the emotional relationship with the object was of an ambivalent nature or because the object cast in that role proved to be too little resistant, resulting in its being relinquished. However, the newly-released libido was "not directed towards another object but drawn back into the Ego"; in other words, it was introjected, which led to a "narcissistic identification" of the Ego with the object it had relinquished.[1] As a result, the object loss had "turned into an Ego loss, and the conflict between the Ego and the beloved into a struggle between Ego criticism and the Ego which had been changed by identification."

In *Freud*'s view, therefore, melancholy – like grief – is, in fact, a "reaction to the real loss of the love object." But in the case of melancholy, in addition to this grief, there is the fact that the emotions, in retreating from the object into the Ego, finally turn against the Ego.[2]

1. S. Freud: *loc. cit.*, p. 437
2. S. Freud: *A General Introduction to Psychoanalysis*, Transl. Joan Riviere. New York, 1920, p. 434f

It seems to me that *Freud* dealt with the problem of melancholy in too narrow a fashion, because he identified it with neurotic depression. *Jung*,[1] on the other hand, saw the problem somewhat differently. He made a precise distinction between true melancholy and psychogenic depression – the latter generally being of neurotic origin. *Jung* sees the difference between melancholy and depression as being that the latter is based on the existence of unconscious figments of the imagination. Exactly the opposite is the case with true melancholy: "The patient has such fantasies because he is in a depressed condition."[2]

According to *Jung*, depression is above all:

> "relative dissociations, a conflict between the Ego and a conflicting force which is based on unconscious contents. These meanings have lost their connection with the psychic whole, to a greater or lesser extent."[3]

From this point of view, it is understandable that *Jung* stresses that the only way to escape from depression is to call up these contents from the unconscious – in other words, to allow oneself to be led by the unconscious, which may express itself in the form of dreams, fantasies, visions and especially in the so-called active imagination. The prerequisite for this, though, is that the depressive should accept his condition and take it seriously, just as *Ficino* did. In this way, he no longer suffers his condition in a purely passive manner but attempts to take an active and reactive part in it. Hence, the contents of the unconscious, which up till now have been themselves unconscious, can be integrated into the Ego.

1. C.G. Jung: *loc. cit.*, p. 213
2. C.G. Jung: *loc. cit.*, p. 214
3. C.G. Jung: *loc. cit.*, p. 190

Our dreamer had minimal artistic talent. Nevertheless, obeying an inner compulsion, he attempted to give creative expression to his fits of melancholy by painting them, which more often than not led to a relaxation of tension and a reduction in the number of periods of depression. Thus there developed a series of paintings, which at first featured negative mother symbols such as crabs and spiders. A long while later, a new series developed, in which the dream picture of Lilith appeared. A further phase began with the dreamer's debate with this picture – because in the interim, he had learnt how to handle his fits of melancholy better, to accept them and also how to give them expression. In the end, periods of spiritual creative activity occurred, usually in connection with melancholic phases.

When this creative activity began, the fits of melancholy generally disappeared. It is true that they did not completely vanish from his life; he remained a lifelong "son of Lilith," but he had learnt how to accept them and gain a positive benefit from them.

3) Lilith and Adam: The Power Struggle

An account of a power struggle between Lilith and Adam is completely unknown to earlier Aggadic, i.e., narrative Jewish literature. It appears for the first time in the Alphabet of ben Sira, which describes the struggle most expressively.

The origin of this story goes back to one of the two widely differing accounts of the creation of woman to be found in Genesis – two passages from different sources.

It is known that modern critical biblical science since *J. Herder, Jean Astruc, Wilhelm M.L. de Wette* and

Julius Wellhausen differentiates between several strands within biblical literature, which were written at different times and by different authors. The oldest strand of the Old Testament is that of the so-called Yahwist (Y), whom many researchers such as *Elias Auerbach, H. Duhm, E. Sellin* and others identify with the High Priest Ebjathar, who lived around 950 B.C. and who was removed from office by King Solomon. The Elohist (E), who lived some 200 years later in the Northern Kingdom of Israel, was followed around 620 B.C. at the time of King Josiah by the Deuteronomist (D), and at the time of the priest Ezra around 440 B.C. by the Priestly Codex (P) – also called the Priestly Writings. In the end, these four sources were brought together by an unknown editor (R) and turned into a more or less unified work (RYEDP).

According to the Yahwist's account, Eve was created from one of Adam's ribs.[1]

According to the Priestly Codex, however, the first human couple was created at one and the same time, on the sixth day.[2] The discrepancy between these two accounts does not seem to have struck commentators until much later on – and even those who noticed the contradiction were unable to explain it. Only after the publication of the ben Sira text did the Rabbis attempt to harmonize the two accounts, by applying the Yahwist's version to Adam and Eve, and that of the Priestly Codex to Adam and Lilith. That is why the Book of Raziel, which dates from considerably later than the ben Sira Midrash, speaks of Lilith

---

1. Gen. 2, 21ff
2. Gen. 1, 26f

as the "first Eve." The term "second Lilith" is never applied to Eve.

Right from the start, there is a violent power struggle between the two partners. But what was this quarrel really about? It was sparked off by disagreements over the position of the two partners during their marital relations. Lilith refused to take the "lower position," whereas Adam insisted on the upper position for himself, basing his claim on the biblical saying, "thy desire shall be to thy husband, and he shall rule over thee."[1] Against this, Lilith backed her own claim with the verse from the Bible which said that they were both made from the earth at the same time. Accordingly, she considered herself as having the same rights as her husband, to be able to act autonomously and to be independent of him – which is why she refused to accept his wish to "lie on top." But while Adam knows exactly what he wants and can also justify this, such is not the case for Lilith. She doesn't explain what she wants. What she really wishes isn't actually in the text.

In contrast, Eve appears as a completely subordinate being, who obviously complies with Adam's wishes without hesitation. She has no problems regarding the position she is supposed to assume.

It is perhaps no coincidence that the Yahwist's historically older version reflects a more patriarchal attitude, whereas the Priestly Codex of some five hundred years later assumes a certain equality between the sexes.

The subsequent Aggadic tradition tends rather towards the Yahwist's version once more, insofar as it attempts to modify the equality between the part-

---

1. Gen. 3, 16

ners. Thus – to take just one example – the Yalqut Re'ubeni, a tract on the fifth Book of Moses which dates from the 17th century, asserts that it really is correct that Adam and Eve were created together from the earth. But whereas God used fresh earth for Adam, He used only dust and dirt to create Lilith.

The power struggle between Adam and Lilith is a reflection of the age-old struggle between the sexes, between the husband's domineering patriarchal atti-tude and the wife's demands for independence and equality. The worldwide female emancipation move-ment has *one* of its starting-points in this Midrash. This problem, which played no part in either the Classical period or the Middle Ages, has become a question of burning importance during the last few hundred years. The modern, self-aware woman at-tempts – insofar as she is not rooted in hereditary tradition and doesn't accept patriarchy as a preor-dained way of life – to free herself more and more from her husband's control and to become an inde-pendent, autonomous being.

When reading the ben Sira text, the modern, psy-chologically complex person endeavors to under-stand the quarrel between the two partners from the standpoint of contemporary depth psychology and to seek both the conscious and, above all, the uncon-scious motives of the warring couple. At first, it may seem a somewhat questionable undertaking to refer figures like Adam and Lilith to the consulting room of a marital therapist or analyst. However, if these figures are viewed as possessing a mythical character, then they reflect a universal and timeless behavior pattern and thus touch on an archetypal problem which also affects modern man. Equally, it is possible to justify viewing Adam and Lilith as a modern, married couple, whose marital conflict is being subjected to a psychological examination. In this case, we are faced with the question: have the two partners behaved correctly from a psychological point of view during their quarrel, or, at least, was there another possible solution to their conflict which might have been more suited to their situation?

The three psychologists referred to earlier investigated this question and attempted – each in her own way – to answer it.

Lewandowski was the first to study the conflict between Adam and Lilith more closely. In so doing, she adopted a careful, rather conservative attitude, in that she supported the view that Adam behaved correctly when he claimed the "upper position" for himself during marital relations. On the other hand Lilith behaved badly because she refused to comply with Adam's wishes; she acted like a woman driven by a self-opinionated animus, i.e., far too "hot-headed and drastic."[1] It should have been her job to understand the problem more from a psychological standpoint, since it was possible for her to conceive of the upper position as "heaven" and the lower one as "earth," i.e., to view the matter symbolically. Her leaving Adam, too, shows "a typical animus manner: using cold reason untempered by sympathetic recognition of the feelings of others."[2] *Lewandowski* concluded that it was exclusively Lilith's responsibility to change her attitude. That she was unable to do this was her own fault.

Vogelsang takes a totally opposing standpoint and follows an overtly feminist line. Although this ren-

1. A. Lewandowski: *loc. cit.*, p. 79
2. A. Lewandowski: *loc. cit.*, p. 80

ders her open to the concerns of the emancipation efforts of the modern feminist movement, her attitude entails a certain prejudice over the question of guilt. She asserts that Adam bears the primary guilt for the disagreement between the two partners, because – so she argues – "from the beginning [he] was trying to assert his superiority and to dominate her, a power play on the part of the masculine."[1] But *Vogelsang* also stresses that "it should be emphasized here that she was not trying to subjugate him. She was trying to maintain her rights."[2] Because Lilith was unable to achieve her legitimate demand, she spoke God's name and escaped Adam by means of a "magic flight."

Lenherr-Baumgartner sees in Lilith and Eve, first and foremost, two differing female types which confront each other.[3] She holds that Adam's demand for the upper position is evolutionarily understandable as a certain male fear of an equal female. Like her predecessor, she also interprets Lilith's departure as a magic flight. In addition, she considers the conflict between the partners as a catastrophe, in that male and female will forever be separate from now on. I would like to remind my readers at this point that the Midrash of ben Sira was written by an unknown man and for men. That is why, in my opinion, the problem is primarily one of the male psyche and concerns the woman only to a limited degree. Indeed, the text of the Midrash cannot be properly understood un-

---

1. E.W. Vogelsang: *loc. cit.*, p. 12
2. E.W. Vogelsang: *idem*
3. In a sermon based on her reading of this study, an American woman Reform rabbi spoke of an Eve-type and a Lilith-type of woman. It would be more correct to speak of an Eve-anima and a Lilith-anima

less we bear in mind the sociological structure of the age when it was written, in which patriarchy was the dominant form of society. The ben Sira text was written down almost a thousand years previously, and may well be based on older oral traditions. It follows that, if we assume that Adam and Lilith made demands of a kind comprehensible to the 20th century, we would be expecting far and away too much from the two partners.

There is another problem. The wife's demand for equality and autonomy must have appeared highly threatening to the male consciousness moulded by the spiritually-patriarchal cultural canons of that age. Clearly, the male consciousness' character mould was not yet adequately consolidated against the prevalent, more matriarchal attitude. *Lenherr-Baumgartner* pinpointed this correctly, when she said:[1] "If one considers the emergence of consciousness, which slowly developed from the unconscious – at first, under the ever-present danger of being swallowed up once again – then one can understand the evolutionary background to Adam's attitude (male fear of an equal female)."[2]

Incidentally, this spiritual-patriarchal moulding not only holds good for the consciousness of Jewish man but is also typical of the whole of Western culture in the Classical period, the Middle Ages and, partially, in modern times. It holds good equally for Christendom, Islam and Judaism. Enough examples of this can be found in the literature of the Church

---

1. The fact that a matriarchal attitude is mentioned in this case does not mean that a sociologically demonstrable matriarchy has ever existed. It is well known that this question is a matter of dispute among ethnologists to the present day
2. C. Lenherr-Baumgartner: *loc. cit.*, p. 19

Fathers, starting with Saints Jerome and John Chrysostom, Clement of Alexandria and on to Saints Augustine and Thomas Aquinas. All of them held the feminine responsible as the true source of all evil. Despite their manifestly patriarchal attitude, neither Judaism nor Islam demonstrates such a condemnation of the feminine.

The dominating attitude of patriarchal man towards the feminine is, at bottom, nothing more nor less than an expression of his deep-seated fears and his uncertainty of womankind. At the same time, behind these fears must also lie a certain fascination.

Fear of the alien unknown generally leads to quite specific defensive reactions, which first become apparent in an attempt to devalue it. This leads in turn to a tendency to dominate and repress the alien.

In this connection, a few questions were raised by the two last-named psychologists. Was Lilith's departure really what modern fairy tale research usually calls a "magic flight"? Indeed, is a flight really involved at all here? Finally, how are we to interpret Lilith's speaking of God's name when she went away?

Before I try to answer these questions, I would like to point out that it is absolutely necessary to follow the ben Sira text word for word during any interpretation. This is not the kind of "Talmudic hairsplitting" or "stubborn belief in words" that Jews are frequently accused of. Accuracy in scientific research is much more an expression of respect and responsibility towards the written word.

So we must first ask ourselves: Is a "magic flight" really involved – indeed, is a flight involved at all? If one reads the ben Sira text carefully, one realizes that there is not a single mention of a *magic flight*. That most competent and undisputed researcher and interpreter of fairy tales, *Marie-Louise von Franz*, has produced an illuminating interpretation of the Siberian fairy tale "The Girl and the Evil Spirit," during the course of which she describes all the characteristics of the magic flight. A prerequisite for it is always a lengthy period of loneliness on the part of the victim. Furthermore, it is characteristic that the victim drops a number of objects behind him- or herself when fleeing. These are meant either to pacify the pursuer or to hold him back from further pursuit for a while. At the same time, the objects represent a kind of sacrificial offering. Hence, "the objects which have been sacrificed generally turn into obstacles for the pursuer."[1] In the fairy tale referred to, the girl drops a comb and a red handkerchief behind her, which turn into a forest and a flame. Absolutely nothing of this nature is to be found in our text.

As a result, we must ask ourselves if a "normal" – i.e., non-magic – flight may perhaps be involved. It should be emphasized that the ben Sira Midrash makes absolutely no mention of a *flight* by Lilith. As far as I know, the variant texts, too, never mention a flight, since none of them contains the verb "to flee."[2] The Hebrew word used is always p-r-ch, which does not mean *to flee* but only ever means *to fly*. If the two above-mentioned writers turned "to fly" into "to flee," therefore, the interpretation was incorrect. Had the author of the ben Sira text wished to say "to flee," the corresponding Hebrew verbs would have been easily available to him.

1. M.-L. von Franz: *An Introduction to the Psychology of Fairy Tales.* Zurich / New York, 1970, p. 132
2. A. ibn Shoshan: *loc. cit.*, cf. p-r-ch

That a flight is not at all the issue here is also clear from the fact that a flight always presupposes a certain danger that the pursuer may chase after the quarry. However, our text does not mention any pursuit of Lilith by Adam.

Even so, it is understandable that *Lenherr-Baumgartner* should speak of a pursuit. In this connection, she bases herself on the book by *Robert von Ranke Graves and Raphael Patai*, who assert: "Because Adam attempted to extract her obedience by force, Lilith became enraged and spoke God's magic name and left him."[1]

It should be stressed that these two authors do not themselves speak of a flight, although this might have been expected from their account. The ben Sira text of the Leyden Codex – on which the two authors expressly base themselves says nothing about the "enraged" uttering of God's "magic" name. Nor is there any mention of an attempt by Adam to rape Lilith. It must be presumed, then, either that the two authors have translated the ben Sira text extremely inaccurately or they have transformed it into a more traditional and freely embellished folk tale. It is evident that such a translation can claim no scientific value. Consequently, the question of what the *uttering of God's name* really means in this instance remains to be answered.

There are a large number of fairy tales in which a divinity, a demon or a helpful spirit is called on by its name. The usual explanation for this implies that the uttering of the secret name equates with a kind of magic ritual, through which the presence of the nu-

---

1. R. von Ranke Graves & R. Patai: *Hebräische Mythologie.* Reinbek bei Hamburg, 1986, p. 80

men can be called up by force or the intervention of supernatural forces can be brought about. The view that to know the name of the spirit one calls up gives one power over it (Rumpelstiltskin motif) is also related to this idea.

Vogelsang obviously also has her eye on these fairy tale motifs, because she comments on the ben Sira text as follows: "It is evident that Lilith's uttering the specific name of God gave her the power to flee from Adam. It was a magical act, being a process by which knowledge of the supernatural can be used to invoke that power to serve one's own purpose."[1] She also tries to support her thesis by stating that, before the children of Israel walked through the Red Sea, "Moses called upon the same ineffable name of God to divide the waters of the Red Sea."[2] The biblical text concerning this incident actually reads: "And Moses stretched out his hand over the sea: and YHWH caused the sea to go back by a strong east wind all that night, and made the sea dry land, and the waters were divided."[3]

Lenherr-Baumgartner is of the same opinion: "But Lilith uses this name for her own personal aims, which equates with a magical misuse and a self-overestimation."[4]

I am not able to endorse this thesis. In any case, the uttering of God's name can be interpreted in quite a different fashion. When the high priest entered the Holy of Holies in the Temple on the Day of

1. E.W. Vogelsang: *loc. cit.*, p. 14
2. E.W. Vogelsang: *loc. cit.*, p. 17f
3. Exod. 14, 21. Later Bible commentaries such as the Midrash rabba, Pirke de Rabbi Eliezer and Raschi also know nothing about Moses' uttering God's name
4. C. Lenherr-Baumgartner: *loc. cit.*, p. 24

Atonement and uttered God's name, the "shem ha'mephorash," before the assembled congregation, it was something quite different from a kind of magic conjuration. Magic invocations and magic practices of all kinds were severely condemned in both biblical and Talmudic times. Whenever they cropped up from time to time among ordinary people, punishment was imposed.

That a Jewish high priest should have used a magic ritual is totally inconceivable, quite apart from the fact that it was also not at all necessary to force YHWH's presence. God's constant presence in His holy temple was never in doubt at any time.

As a result, I ask myself whether the uttering of God's name may not have another significance, that might be more in keeping with the spirit of this event.

It seems to me that speaking YHWH's name might rather express what could be called a "giving of a sign." On that day on which, after confessing his sins, the high priest reconciles himself with his God, it is perfectly conceivable that he wished to "give a sign" that the reconciliation had been consummated, which freed both him and all the people from the burden of their sins. It seems to me that, in this case, the uttering of God's name has neither a *magic* nor a *symbolic* significance. As a rule, the latter is the expression of a more half-conscious occurrence. On the other hand, a "giving of a sign" is a universally known and consciously perceived occurrence, which is of a more *semiotic* significance. The thesis of semiotic significance can be supported by two examples. A parallel from the Christian cultural group presents itself in the form of the act of sacrifice during the mass. When the officiating priest speaks the words of consecration, the transformation of the sacrificial offerings and the presence of Christ is guaranteed eo ipso. However, in no way does this involve a magic ritual, by means of which the transformation and the presence of Christ would be enforced. As is continually and unanimously stressed, the priest is merely an instrument of service in the sacred act – and the words of consecration do not bring about the transformation or the presence of the Son of God, which is exclusively a spontaneous act of mercy on God's part. By speaking the words of consecration, the priest gives a sign for the voluntary transformation of bread and wine into the body and blood of Christ, as well as for His presence in this mystery.

A further historical occurrence points in the same direction. Around the middle of the 17th century, there arose within the ranks of Judaism a redemption movement linked to the name of Sabbatai Sevi. This young Kabbalist was deeply convinced of his messianic mission. At the age of only twenty-two, he dared to utter the shem ha'mephorash in front of the assembled Jewish congregation in the synagogue of his home town of Smyrna. This, too, was no symbolic act, as I myself first assumed.[1] Rather, by so doing, he attempted to give a sign that the time of redemption had arrived and that he was the promised Messiah. The whole congregation also took it in this sense. The tragic consequences did not fail to materialize. I also take Lilith's speaking of God's name before her departure as a conscious "giving of a sign." By doing this, she wishes to make it clear that

---

1. S. Hurwitz: "Sabbatai Zvi" in *Psyche und Erlösung*. Zurich, 1983, p. 93

she is not prepared to accept her husband Adam's patriarchal superiority.

It might be conceivable that Lilith's departure is the result of her realization that a further struggle would be pointless. Consequently, I wouldn't at all like to subject myself to specifying whether it was the result of resignation or of prudent reflection, since I cannot push through my claims. So it is better to quit the field... I would like to underline, though, that these observations are purely speculative and do not come out of the text itself.

What does it really mean when Lilith "flies into the air"? The one certainty is that, as a result, she loses contact with Adam and thus also the possibility of a further quarrel. Naturally, the possibility presents itself of interpreting the flight into the air as a kind of inflation, since in this way Lilith ceases to be earthbound. But I would like to refrain from further speculation and keep to the text.

When it is said in this connection that Lilith goes to the Red Sea or into the desert, it is not enough to amplify these two terms and to investigate their symbolic character. We need to ask: what do the Red Sea and the desert mean for a self-aware Jew? Remember, the author of the ben Sira text was a Jew and was addressing himself to a Jewish readership.

First of all, we should point out that the *Red Sea* and its surrounding area is a landscape of exceptional beauty. The passage of the children of Israel took place at the so-called Sea of Reeds, the lakeland district that, at this time, was connected to the Gulf of Suez. For the Jews, the Red Sea is characterized by this historic event, which took place about 1200 B.C. The Hebrew tribes who fled from the oppression of the construction-mad Ramses II found themselves in a life-threatening situation. Behind them were the pursuing Egyptian troops, before them were the waters of the Red Sea. Here, they experienced the miracle of salvation from extreme need, of which Israel's victory song tells.[1] Thus, the Red Sea has a dual character in this context: it is a place of danger but also of a divine miracle that proved to be life-saving.

The situation is exactly the same as regards the *desert*. The sojourn in the desert, be it in Judaea, Sinaï or the desert round the Padua Hills in California, provides the observer with a uniquely attractive experience. Also, of course, the desert has an added significance to a Jew as the place from which he originated. The spiritual structure of the semi-nomadic tribes of Israel was largely moulded by their sojourn in the desert. True, the rich arable land to the West was always the goal of their longing. But at the same time, they despised the Canaanitic farmers for their earthbound sedentariness.

Whereas a partial interbreeding with the Canaanites occurred in the northern kingdom of Israel, the nomadic ideal remained preeminent in the southern kingdom of Judah.

The desert is also closely associated with the moment at which the threat of the Fata Morgana and self-loss is at its greatest. It is connected as well with the long sojourn of the tribes of Israel following Moses' hearing God's call from the burning bush and His appearance to him on Mount Sinaï. In later times, it was the prophets above all who upheld the desert ideal and extolled the simple, honorable and straightforward character of those who lived in the

1. Exod. 15, 1ff

desert. The Recabite sect went still further, in that their way of life resembled that of the Nomads.

Like the Red Sea, the desert has an ambivalent character, representing both the place of origin and also the desire to escape from it. Like the Red Sea, too, the desert also symbolizes the unconscious, with its ambivalent character.

That Lilith loses a hundred of her children each day as a result of her disobedience towards YHWH is the punishment of a patriarchal Father God who is not prepared to accept female independence. The behavior of the two partners, Adam and Lilith, was – as we have seen – assessed differently by the three psychologists. However, it doesn't seem very meaningful to me to carry out an evaluation at all. I consider it more important to try to understand the behavior of Adam and Lilith.

Nowadays, a marital therapist would probably try to effect a compromise in this quarrel about "position," either by suggesting they should take it in turns to claim the upper position, or that they should consider the possibility of alternative positions to "on top" and "underneath." But neither Adam nor Lilith entertains such considerations. Adam bases himself on his supposedly unequivocal right, while for her part, Lilith claims her perfect right to equality. This quarrel cannot be settled in a sensible fashion because "they don't listen to each other."

Although I may lay myself open to the suspicion of defending a patriarchal attitude, it seems to me that Adam should not give in, if he doesn't want to put his masculinity at risk. Nevertheless, Lilith's behavior is also completely understandable – though she is far and away in advance of her time in her demands. Her claim to autonomy and independence repre-

sents a first – if unsuccessful – attempt to do away
with the traditional supremacy of men. Because in
those days such an attempt was doomed to failure,
Lilith was left with only two choices: either to go back
to Adam, which would have entailed total submis-
sion, or to go away. This means that the conflict will
first of all be pushed into the unconscious.

Lenherr-Baumgartner considered this separation of
the masculine from the feminine to be a catastrophe,
because "Adam's arrogance towards the feminine is
just as disastrous as Lilith's subsequent refusal to
return."[1]

I cannot go along with this opinion. It seems psychologically more sensible to me to put aside a conflict which is insoluble, for the time being, rather
than to work through it at all costs. In such cases,
there is always the hope that, in the course of a
lengthy maturation process, the conflict can be resolved later or will lose importance as other problems come into the foreground. Lilith's attempt to
win independence for herself appears to be the reason why, nowadays, she has become the symbol of the
struggle for female independence throughout the
world. Indirectly, in fact, she reflects a side of the
modern woman who wants to bring about a change
in the existing understanding of the roles of men
and women. Nowadays, self-aware men are also beginning to recognize this and to debate the question
seriously.

The number of women dealing with this problem
from the psychological standpoint is growing continually. Thus, *Judith Plaskow Goldenberg*[2] and her circle

---

1. C. Lenherr-Baumgartner: *loc. cit.*, p. 18
2. J. Plaskow Goldenberg: "The Coming of Lilith" in *Religion and Sexism*. Brattleboro, 1974, p. 342ff

have produced a collectively elaborated fantasy, in which Lilith and Eve meet and become reconciled. I find it far more valuable, though, that individual men and women are tackling the problem in both their active imaginations and their external discussions. It is obvious that, as a result, dreams are also taken into consideration.

While this does not in the least suggest that the women's movement has no justification, it does seem to me that any attempt to establish a kind of matriarchy in place of the crumbling patriarchy of our day would represent an unfortunate regression into a psychologically long-outdated attitude. But it can be presumed that, with the progressive development of consciousness of men and women and the growing realization of the legitimate demands of women, extreme forms of discussion will disappear once again and will simply be seen as temporary phenomena.

4) Fear and Fascination

At the beginning of this chapter, I mentioned that our dreamer's attitude towards the picture of Lilith was indecisive in that, while he was intensely fascinated by the dream image, he was also seized by an almost panic-stricken fear. A personal problem suffered by the dreamer is not the sole reason for this. Such an ambivalent attitude generally characterizes both archaic man and children. Each experiences the outside world as something powerful and dangerous, even life-threatening. But the weak and easily-tired Ego often feels defenseless faced with the inner world, the unconscious and its frequently terrifying figures and dangers. The sensation of being threatened is particularly pronounced among highly introverted people and those who have remained young for far too long. For a man, the sensation of being threatened from outside or inside – or from both sides at the same time – only dissolves when his Ego-consciousness is reinforced and he has found his masculine maturity and roots deep within himself. Even then, such primeval fears are liable to resurface from time to time. They tend to manifest themselves in a fear of women and of the unconscious – personified either in the mother or in the anima.

The problem of a man's fear of women was investigated by *Karen Horney*,[1] who was originally a pupil of the *Freudian* school. She attempted to find the reasons for it in the man's childhood development. But in *Horney*, unlike *Freud*, what is involved is less a fear of castration (i.e., the boy's fear of his father, which prevents him committing incest with his mother) than a "reaction to the threat to his self-esteem." For the growing boy, this threat may arise from frustrating experiences with his mother, who denies herself to him, thus damaging his masculine self-esteem.

However, it seems to me that *Horney*, in spite of several interesting approaches, views the problem somewhat too narrowly and tries to reduce it to a purely personal way of looking at things. In such situations, it is not merely the child's own mother who is involved but, to a far greater extent, all that the mother symbolizes for the growing child: the unconscious in both its positive and negative maternal aspects – in other words, the Mother Archetype, as *Jung*[2] called it in many of his works.

1. K. Horney: "Die Angst vor der Frau" in *Internationale Zeitschrift für Psychoanalyse*. Vienna, 1932, Vol. XVIII, p. 5ff
2. C.G. Jung: "Psychological Aspects of the Mother Archetype" in *The Archetypes and the Collective Unconscious*. Princeton & London, 1959, CW, Vol. IX, p. 81ff

Building on Jung's train of thought, *Neumann*[1] carried out further investigations into the fear of the feminine. He distinguishes between the male child's fear of the "elemental character" of the feminine – in other words, the mother aspect – and the fear of the "transformation character," i.e., the anima aspect. Such fears go back to various causes, one of which is a disturbed original relationship between the child and his mother, who at the same time represents the embodiment of the mother archetype for the child. A further cause stems from the disruption of normal development in connection with the transition from the matriarchal to the patriarchal phase. At a later stage, such fears of the anima appear in connection with the dangers of the fight against the dragon, which is a prerequisite for the freeing of the anima from the mother archetype.

Assuming this assumption is correct, these fears come far less from one's own mother than from the superior strength of the mother archetype. In both the child and archaic man, fear is, in normal circumstances, a completely natural occurrence. It represents the weak Ego's defense against the dissolving tendency of the unconscious – which is why an introverted man will often build up a whole system of defense mechanisms and safety precautions, as *Alfred Adler* has impressively shown.

Even modern man, whose consciousness is developed and to some extent consolidated, is frequently the victim of such primeval fears. However, according to *Neumann*, these also represent an:

1. E. Neumann: "Die Angst vor dem Weiblichen" in *Die Angst.* Studien aus dem C.G. Jung Institut, Zurich. Zurich, 1958/59, Vol. X, p. 81ff

"... incentive to such development [of consciousness]. Vital components in the growth of the ego and in the evolution of consciousness, culture, religion, art, and science spring from the urge to overcome this fear by giving it concrete expression. It is therefore quite wrong to reduce it to personal or environmental factors and to seek to get rid of it in that way."[1]

The upshot is that fear of the feminine, whether it approaches him from outside as a woman or from inside as mother and anima, is most certainly not unfounded. In a man, it is based as well, among other things, on an unconscious intuition of the emotional wildness, passion and lack of restraint which is frequently characteristic of the feminine. Consequently, the fear of becoming enslaved by a woman or by the mother anima image is understandable.

On the other hand, fear is only the reverse of a corresponding, equally strong, fascination. The man finds it difficult to elude this fascination, which comes either from a woman or – as with every archetype – even from the mother image and the anima. So it is both fear and fascination which, with the utmost difficulty, fashion the man's debate with the feminine. This can be seen clearly from the example of the dreamer cited earlier.

Depending on whether fear or fascination prevails, certain types of behavior and reactions occur. If fear takes on extreme forms, then repression and, eventually, separation – in our case, from the inner figure – may result. For the man, this separation from the feminine, especially if it lasts for a long time, involves severe psychological damage, because

1. E. Neumann: *The Origin and History of Consciousness.* Princeton & London, 1954, p. 41

in this way he remains separated from life or from his Eros and emotions. As far as the anima is concerned, though, this archetype will as a rule constellate sooner or later and assert itself through its inner dynamism and intensity, as was also the case with our dreamer.

If the man remains unaware of this development, however, he will be seized by his anima and become the victim of his own emotionalism and – should he be the intellectual type – by his base feelings: he will become moody, touchy or ambitious, and, in the worst cases, quite effeminate. According to *Jung*

> "... the unconscious anima is a creature without relationships, an autoerotic being whose one aim is to take total possession of the individual. When this happens to a man, he becomes strangely womanish in the worst sense."[1]

A further possibility arises from projections of the anima, through which the man gets into all kinds of external entanglements and relationship difficulties. If such a projection should fall on a woman similar to Lilith – as in our case – then, sooner or later, the man will be confronted either with her seductive side or, perhaps more dangerously, with her desire for power. In this conflict, he can either fail or grow, depending on whether he submits or attempts to assert himself and thus develops his masculinity. But the self-assertion and self-protection should not go so far as to deny the feminine its due worth.

On the contrary, only the man who went through his anima experience in a self-aware manner, and

---

1. C.G. Jung: "The Psychology of Transference" in *Specific Problems of Psychotherapy*. Princeton & London, 1954, CW, Vol. XVI, p. 295

thus won his virility in a mature fashion, is at all capable of integrating his anima.

If fascination gains the upper hand, the man may eventually identify himself with the archetype, which can also lead to highly unfavorable character changes. This becomes especially clear when he falls under the spell of Lilith's Ishtar aspect.

But women themselves are not exempt from ambivalent feelings, which alternate between fear and fascination vis à vis the archetype. In their case, too, fear of their own destructive Lamashtû aspect can lead to its repression and, in certain cases, even to its separation. In this event, the woman's consciousness contains the image of a kindly, helpful, protective and caring mother who is life-preserving and life-giving, whereas in her unconscious the picture of a terrifying, devouring mother dominates – a situation of which neuropsychology can provide many examples.

Since, in the case of Lilith, a being of the same sex is involved, it seems to me that the fear of separation is somewhat smaller for a woman than for a man. Instead, the fear of identification is greater. If a woman identifies herself with her Lamashtû aspect, this has a highly destructive effect on her immediate surroundings, above all. In particular, she will try to keep her children away from life, to dominate them and to prevent their development into independent personalities. As a result, the children's creative abilities cannot develop, either. But such an attitude finally rebounds on her, in that, especially if she has no children, her own creativity is destroyed. As in the Lilith myth, she strangles her own spiritual children if she cannot find any strange children. She can do this all the more easily when the woman's animus parrots the chattering of the collective masculine consciousness, which attempts to deny a woman any creativity whatsoever.

In contrast, when the woman identifies herself with the Ishtar aspect of Lilith, her nature is somewhat negatively moulded. There develops an excessive Eros and an attitude that may be Lilith-like.

According to *Jung,* such a woman loves

> "... romantic and sensational episodes for their own sake, and is interested in married men, less for themselves than for the fact that they are married and so give her an opportunity to wreck a marriage, that being the whole point of her maneuver. Once the goal is attained, her interest evaporates for lack of any maternal instinct and then it will be someone else's turn."[1]

The Lilith-like woman goes through life internally unmoved and unconscious of her own actions, without in the slightest accounting to herself for what she might have started. She tries to reflect the anima of the man with whom she has a relationship, with the unconscious intention of gaining control of him. Like Lilith and the Arabic Karina, it gives her satisfaction to push herself between husband and wife and to disrupt or destroy their relationship. She succeeds in this mainly because she knows how to play the part of a desirable girl and seduce all men by appealing to their protective instincts. In this, she behaves like Lilith in her Ishtar aspect, wherein she "sleeps with every man in the world," as one Kabbalist puts it.[2]

1. C.G. Jung: "Psychological Aspects of the Mother Archetype" in *The Archetypes and the Collective Unconscious.* Princeton & London, 1959, CW, IX, p. 89
2. G. Scholem: "Lilith ve'Na'amah liphne ha'melech Shlomo" in *Peraqim chadashim me'injenei Ashmedai ve'Lilith.* TZ, Jerusalem, 1947/48, Vol. XIX, p. 174

As a rule, though, the Lilith-like woman is not totally destructive. By disrupting a problematic marriage, she can in fact create moral conflicts which, in turn, constitute a starting point for a change not only in the marriage but above all in the married couple themselves – one which can lead to change and development in their consciousness. On top of this, she is often caught up – against her will – in the disruption she has caused and is forced to take part in the conflict, to develop and to learn a bit of self-awareness. However, if she avoids this challenge, she will have to pay the corresponding price and, sooner or later, fall victim to a neurosis.

5) The Second Encounter: An Active Imagination

In dealing with the dream experience which afforded our dreamer a first encounter with the figure of Lilith, we endeavored – by means of association and amplification – to create a context which would provide a clarification of the dream picture and an understanding of the dreamer's emotions.

In the following section, we will turn to the question of what this experience signified for the dreamer, what kind of effect it had on his personal life, and what were the eventual consequences for him and his inner development.

Some five years after his first encounter with Lilith, the dreamer had an external anima experience. As was only to be expected, his projection fell on a girl who was very similar to Lilith. She was an attractive young woman who attempted to ensnare the dreamer with all the feminine charms at her disposal. Her excessive Eros had ensured that, even in her earliest youth, she had had friendships with numerous men – generally married. These friendships always ended at the exact moment when the problem of a psychological relationship and an attendant dawning of consciousness arose, because she was adept at avoiding conflict and invariably drew back at the critical moment.

The experience implied a difficult moral conflict for the dreamer. But he sensed, unconsciously, that he *had* to go through it. True, his still all-too-rational consciousness tried to persuade him that what was involved was "only" a projection. Nevertheless, the fascination remained. While he was aware that he had become the victim of a fascination based on the projection of his own feminine side, this insight did not help him in the slightest to extricate himself from the entanglement. Had he understood the meaning of the dream picture at the time, he would have been forewarned or at least prepared in advance for this experience. But revenge was exacted for the fact that he had obviously not taken his dream experience seriously enough, in that he was now also confronted externally with a Lilith figure. So this conflict found him somewhat unprepared and almost proved to be his undoing. The Lilith anima very subtly attempted to win the dreamer for herself. But as the erotic encounter began to change into a psychological disagreement, she instinctively sensed that the problem was beginning to disturb her personally. Instead of taking on her conflict and working through it, she evaded it and suppressed it.

For the dreamer, though, there was a gradual diminution in the projection. He recognized that the woman who had approached him externally was a reflection of his own irrational side, of his anima. As a result, he realized not only the existence of his own feelings but also gained a deeper relationship with his Eros.

In this development of consciousness, something else was also brought home to the dreamer. The woman had grown up in a strongly Christian environment. He began to ask himself what the significance was of his encountering a Christian anima. On this occasion, he remembered an earlier dream that he now understood more clearly:

> "I am with my father in a synagogue, praying. As we are both leaving, I see that the back of the synagogue is a Catholic church."

The dreamer's association arose from the fact that he was born and brought up in a Roman Catholic town. The church was near his parents' house and the presbytery was just opposite it. Personal relations with the priest were of the best. The annual Corpus Christi procession made a deep impression on the sensitive dreamer. So it was not surprising that the Christian milieu influenced him, although he was always aware of his Jewishness and reacted positively to its spiritual merits.

What emerges from the dream is that behind the front-facing façade, that is, his *conscious* Jewish behavior, lies a Catholic church – in other words, that his *unconscious* attitude was influenced by Christianity. The parallelism of the two sacral areas might well point to certain religious parallel developments which, independently of each other, can be detected in both Judaism and Christianity. Among these, to give just one example, belongs the Christian view on the development of the image of God, as expressed in the teaching on incarnation. In the Jewish sphere, it could be held that this finds its equivalent in the

Kabbalistic teaching on the development of en Sof into the Sefiroth. The difference between these two beliefs stems from the fact that, from the Christian point of view, the incarnation is a unique, historically comprehensible truth, whereas according to the Kabbalistic version, this process of development is continuous – and, indeed, takes place within the divine sphere.[1]

The second encounter with Lilith does not involve a dream experience but what *Jung* calls an *active imagination*, which involves a method of introspection that he developed.[2] This method of extracting unconscious material from the depths of the unconscious, according to *Marie-Louise von Franz*, comes into play

> "... when either excess pressure is exerted on the unconscious, that is too many dreams and fantasies occur, or, just the opposite, when dream life is blocked."[3]

It is not that the active imagination is an unrestrained, constant fantasizing. *Jung* says that a fantasy is

> "... more or less your own invention, and remains on the surface of personal things and conscious expectations. But active imagination, as the term denotes, means that the images have a life of their own and that

1. Cf. C.G. Jung: Letter to James Kirsch in *Letters of C.G. Jung*. Princeton & London, 1972, Vol. II, p. 91ff
2. C.G. Jung: *The Transcendent Function*. Princeton & London, 1960, CW, Vol. VIII, p. 68
3. M.-L. von Franz: "Die aktive Imagination in der Psychologie C.G. Jungs" in W. Bitter: *Meditation in Religion und Psychotherapie*. Stuttgart, 1958, p. 143; now available in M.-L. von Franz, *Psychotherapie*, Einsiedeln, 1990.

the symbolic events even develop according to their own logic..."[1]

In active imagination, there is a kind of "fading out" of consciousness, bringing about a condition which *Pierre Janet* describes as "abaissement du niveau mental."

Meditation techniques of various kinds have been widely known from time immemorial. For example, there are mystical texts from *Sufism*, which recommend meditation on the name of Allah until a kind of trance condition is reached. Within the *Kabbalah*, too, particularly in the school of thought represented by *Abraham Abulafia* and his disciples, meditative practices are recommended which can lead one to reach a state of ecstasy. In a manuscript work by one of *Abulafia's* disciples, three different ways of attaining mystical ecstasy are distinguished:[2] the *universal* way of the Sufic mystic, the *philosophical* way, which is based on reason, and the *Kabbalistic* way. The latter is praised as the pinnacle of them all. Then follow instructions to meditate on the four letters of the divine name YHWH, to permutate and combine its letters until they acquire a life of their own.

In modern times, too, many different techniques for meditation and introspection have been developed, both in religious circles and in psychotherapy. For this kind of introspection as well, a specific object is adapted for the meditative purpose, e.g., the cross itself in the so-called meditation on the cross. In the case of active imagination, however, the choice of

1. C.G. Jung: "The Tavistock Lectures" (1935), Lecture V (Discussion) in *The Symbolic Life*, CW Vol. XVIII, Princeton & London, 1976, p. 171
2. G. Scholem: *Major Trends in Jewish Mysticism*. New York, 1961, p. 147

object on which to meditate is generally left to the unconscious. If one concentrates on the unconscious, an inner picture or dream fragment emerges. After a period of intensive concentration, this begins to develop a life of its own. According to *Jung*:

> "... one holds on to this picture by concentrating all one's attention on it. As a rule, it changes as it is brought to life through the mere fact of being observed. From this, there develops a chain of fantasy images which gradually assume a dramatic character. To this end, it is essential that the observer be drawn into the dramatic action, that he conducts himself in the fantasy as he would doubtless conduct himself in reality."[1]

When dealing with active imagination, it is especially important to distinguish scrupulously between what belongs to the analysand's conscious experience and knowledge and where imagination goes beyond personal barriers and ventures into the realm of the archetypes. The analysand knew this, which is why he behaved at first in a somewhat cautious and sceptical fashion, unlike his reaction to the Lilith dream. He asked himself, quite correctly, if in this instance there really was a true imagination and thus a manifestation of the unconscious, or if his imagination was perhaps only a product of conscious fantasizing. Between the two events, he had not only acquired a certain experience in his dealings with dreams but had also developed an instinct for the genuineness of the inner event. As a result, he was

---

1. C.G. Jung: "The Relations between the Ego and the Unconscious" in *Two Essays on Analytical Psychology*. Princeton & London, 1953, CW, Vol. VII

perfectly capable of distinguishing between the personal and the suprapersonal. The *imagination* goes:

"I am hunting for the old Jewish cemetery in Toledo, where I am supposed to be deciphering certain old gravestones. But the cemetery no longer exists. In its place stands the new, magnificent cathedral. The former Jewish quarter round the present cathedral is no longer there, either. I go on into another quarter – also Jewish – and ask various people about the Rabbi of Toledo. One of them calls over a girl of about twenty, the Rabbi's granddaughter. She is a beautiful girl, with enormous dark eyes and red hair, which flows down behind her back. She is wearing a scarlet dress. I ask her what her name is. At first, she is somewhat embarrassed, then she says: 'My name is Simcha, but my friends just call me Lilith.' I ask her smilingly: 'If you really are Lilith, where have you hidden your wings?' She blushes with embarrassment and says nothing. Then she takes me to her grandfather.

I ask the Rabbi of Toledo: 'Rabbi, tell me, what is the most important thing I still have to learn in my life?' The Rabbi thinks for a long while, gives me a piercing look and smiles: 'The most important thing that you still have to learn in your life is how to dance properly.' I stare at him in astonishment and am unable to understand exactly what he means. So he calls his granddaughter and they both begin to instruct me in the 'correct' way to dance, with Simcha-Lilith dancing with me and the Rabbi looking on and clapping the beat for us. The dance proceeds as follows: first, three slow steps to the left, then one back to the right and so on, until a full circle has been danced. Then the dance is repeated in reverse order. The Rabbi counts the beat: 'One-two-three and one,' because the fourth step is the most important.

At the end of the dance ceremony, the girl hands me a golden ring which I immediately put on. The Rabbi presents me with a Kabbalistic book, which I am to give to a friend of his who is a Rabbi in Jerusalem."

Commentary:

The imagination takes us to the Toledo of the end of the 14th century, i.e., to a time when the city was still under Arab rule and had a flourishing Jewish community. Here we must ask ourselves exactly why the imagination chose the town of Toledo[1] and what symbolic value this town held for the dreamer. In addition to this, we must ask what the status of the symbol of the *city* actually is.

The analysand's associations revealed that he had been fascinated by Spain since his childhood. In literature, he was acquainted with both *Franz Grillparzer*'s tragedy "Die Jüdin von Toledo" ("The Jewess of Toledo") and with *Lion Feuchtwanger*'s novel "Spanische Ballade" ("Spanish Ballad"). The historically authenticated love story between King Alfonso VIII and the beautiful Jewess, Rahel, which is mentioned in these two pieces of literary evidence, plays no part. Even so, the analysand remembered that, according to an oral family tradition, his forebears originally came from Spain and only emigrated from there after the edict of King Ferdinand of Aragon and Isabella of Castile in 1492. Many of his ancestors lived in Bohemia and Germany. Some of them were leading Kabbalists during the Thirty Years War; others were Hassidic leaders in the 18th century.

During his repeated visits to Spain, the analysand had never failed to visit Toledo, with which he had a

---

1. Cf. the Toledo dream in C.G. Jung: "The Tavistock Lectures" (1935), Lecture IV, in *The Symbolic Life*, CW Vol. XVIII, Princeton, 1976, p. 121f, in which, however, other aspects are in the foreground

specially close relationship. He used to wander through the winding alleys of the old town with the inescapable feeling that he had already lived there before. Perhaps this was an example of the experience generally known as déjà-vu. In the magnificent synagogue built by the treasurer of King Pedro I, the Cruel, he had an experience: an inner voice demanded that he recite the old Jewish prayer for the dead (Kaddish) for the many martyrs who had found death in Spain and Germany for the sake of their faith. After the Jews were driven out of Spain, this synagogue was handed over to the Order of Calatrava, which consecrated it to the Virgin Mary as "El Tránsito de Nuestra Señora." To this day, one can still find a few gravestones of knights of this order set into the synagogue's floor.

Toledo is a city whose origins are completely lost in the mists of time. It is true that Jewish tradition had linked the city's name from early on with the Hebrew word toledoth, which means something like family tree or line – because this tradition had it that the city was founded by the descendants of Noah. In reality, though, Toledo was founded by the Celtiberians. Around 200 B.C., it was captured by the Romans, who called it Toletum. At first, it was merely a humble provincial city. But by the time of the migration of the peoples, in particular after the invasion of the Visigoth tribes, Toledo had acquired a leading position. Under King Leovigild, its status was raised to that of royal residence. By 400 A.D., the city had already become a religious center and the seat of a bishop, who was later to be Primate of Spain. When, in 586 A.D., King Reccared abandoned Arianism, which the Visigoths had embraced, and converted to Roman Catholicism, this became the sole established religion of Spain. The numerous Church Councils held in Toledo took decisions that influenced political matters as well as Church affairs.

With the conversion to Catholicism came the first wave of Jewish persecutions, which ended only when the city was captured by the Arabs in 711 A.D. Under Arab rule, culture blossomed, with Arabs, Christians and Jews taking an equal part. At the end of the Reconquista (the retaking of Spain by the Christians), Toledo was made the seat of the Kings of Spain. Under Charles V, it became an imperial city, retaining its importance as a religious center even when Philip II later transferred the royal residence to Madrid.

Toledo is the capital of New Castile, which, along with Catalonia, was the most important center of Jewish mysticism.[1] There were Kabbalists such as *Todros Abulafia* and *Josef ibn Waqar* living in Toledo, *Isaac* and *Jacob ha'Cohen* in Soria, *Josef Gikatila* in Medinaceli, and *Moses de Burgos* and *Moses de León* in Guadalajara and Avila.

The city of Toledo is almost circular in design and lies in the center of Spain on a hill bounded on three sides by the River Tagus. The Visigoth and Arab defensive walls, of which parts are still standing, are breached by four gates. Of the great Spanish cathedrals, those of Toledo, Burgos and León are the most impressive. Toledo's was constructed at the beginning of the 13th century in a square which belonged to a Jewish quarter. The cathedral itself rests on the foundations of a mosque, which in its turn was originally a Visigoth place of worship. It is not only the

---

1. Y. Baer: *A History of Jews in Christian Spain.* Philadelphia, 1961, Vol. I, p. 50ff

center of the whole city but also symbolizes the ecclesia militans, which proved a driving factor during the Reconquista. In addition, it is a symbol of a Christian Imperium and, above all, of the Western Christian culture.

The circular *city* is, psychologically speaking, a symbol of the psychic whole. The circle divided by the cross is the universal ground plan for all archaic cities, as is apparent from numerous finds in Europe, Asia and pre-Columbian America. When the Romans founded a city, they used to plough a circular furrow, which was then divided into four "quarters." Thus, the quartered city is a symbol of the self. The image of the heavenly Jerusalem was also employed in that sense. This symbol first appears in the *Talmud*,[1] and came down to *Paul*[2] and thus to the *New Testament*,[3] and finally to various *Gnostic* sects.[4] The heavenly Jerusalem is the archetype of the earthly Jerusalem and, according to Jewish tradition, will be sent down by God at the time of the Messiah to replace the earthly version, which has been destroyed.

According to old Jewish tradition, the earthly *Jerusalem*, too, to which the dreamer is supposed to take the book and the ring at the end of his imagination, is the central point of the whole country, which in turn is the "navel" of the world. In Jerusalem itself, the place where the Temple used to stand is the center of the city. So it could be said that both Toledo and Jerusalem symbolize the self, one in its Christian, the other in its Jewish aspect.

---

1. B.T.: Traktat Ta'anit 5a; Traktat Sukka 51b
2. Paul: Epistle to the Galatians 4, 26
3. Rev.: 21, 2
4. H. Leisegang: *Die Gnosis*. Leipzig, 1924, p. 140

The dreamer is searching for the old Jewish cemetery, in order to decipher gravestones. Clearly, by so doing, he is trying to establish a link with his people and his ancestors. But it isn't possible to do so by this means, because gravestones are dead matter. In the event, he doesn't find the gravestones but instead meets a living girl.

Compared with the dream picture in which Lilith first appeared, a completely different scenario is portrayed. In the first place, the whole *atmosphere* of the imagination is already much more harmonious, relaxed and serene. Fear and fascination have disappeared almost completely. The dreamer has also developed a much more natural attitude towards the people and events concerned. He is no longer a purely passive observer but takes as active a part in events as he would in reality.

The anima figure which appears in this case is called *Simcha,* which in Hebrew means "joy." Thus, she symbolizes the dreamer's passion for life which left him because it was linked to the unconscious anima. At the same time, she is also *Lilith,* although she has undergone an important transformation. No longer is she an archaic goddess or a demonic figure corresponding to the dreamer's primitive natural and instinctive anima, which neither speaks to the dreamer nor attempts to relate to him. Here, the anima has taken on human shape – which means, from a psychological point of view, that she has been to a great extent brought closer to consciousness.

There is no sense in speculating whether the dreamer's consciousness has changed since the first appearance of the Lilith picture and, as a result, the unconscious anima image has also begun to change, or whether the exact opposite has occurred, with the anima image being the first to change and the dreamer's consciousness following suit as a consequence. Both processes occur as parallels.

The girl Simcha-Lilith attempts neither to seduce the dreamer nor to gain control of him. But although the anima is portrayed as a simple, natural girl, she is nevertheless not a figure from the dreamer's conscious world. She still has a pair of wings somewhere, stored away in a secret place. The fact that the girl is embarrassed by the mention of these wings may be a sign that, having now developed her human side, she no longer wishes to be reminded of her archaic, demonic origins, which she has finally cast off.

The *red hair* and *scarlet dress* point to the dreamer's developing emotionalism and related feelings. In the Zohar, too, Lilith has red hair and a scarlet dress.[1] The dreamer's original far-reaching unconsciousness has changed, or – alchemically speaking – the rubedo has now developed from the nigredo of the first encounter, leading to a certain stimulation of the unconscious.

The anima figure of the second encounter is considerably *younger* than that of the Lilith dream. This means that, in the interim, there has been a change in the dreamer's consciousness. As a rule, it is known that a man who remains childishly immature has a more maternal anima, whereas a man whose consciousness is too old has that of a young girl. Both figures compensate for the dreamer's too one-sided attitude. The younger girl shows that our dreamer is clearly undergoing an internal maturation process.

1. Zohar I 148a b

It is the anima figure that leads the dreamer to her grandfather. We see that the seductress has become a companion and spiritual guide, since she leads the dreamer to another, equally archetypal figure. For the Rabbi of Toledo is the spiritual leader of the community and thus a kind of *wise old man*. As an "archetype of meaning," as *Jung*[1] calls him, he knows the dreamer's hidden thoughts which he has to fulfill. These secret thoughts are made manifest by the ensuing dance ceremony.

The *dance* in this case is less the expression of an erotic situation – although coming close to it, since the dreamer dances with the girl – than a ritual act of the greatest numinous significance. Dances play an important role in the initiation rites of primitive peoples. They rehearse them for hours to the sound of their bush drums.

The dance follows a movement which leads the dreamer and the anima first to the left, and then, when the circle has been closed, to the right – that is, against consciousness.

What is involved is a kind of round dance, during which a mandala is performed. On one count, this is a protective circle; at the same time, it represents the unity of the personality, in which feeling has now found its rightful place. The *rhythm* of the dance also points in this direction: the movement is executed as three steps to the left and one to the right. This recalls the so-called axiom of *Maria Prophetissa,* which is repeatedly mentioned in alchemical texts, and which also talks about the fourth, the cause of the

---

1. C.G. Jung: "Archetypes of the Collective Unconscious" in *The Archetypes and the Collective Unconscious.* Princeton & London, 1959, CW, IX, p. 37

one and the whole.[1] Plainly, what is referred to here is the problem of the fourth, i.e., the fourth base function of feeling, which the dreamer now has to realize.

As they part, the anima gives our dreamer a ring, which has dual significance. It is the round, the unity. It is also the expression of a close inner bond and attachment. During the Jewish wedding ceremony, the bridegroom puts a ring on the bride's finger with the words: "With this ring you are bound to me in holy matrimony according to the law of Moses and Israel."

The Kabbalistic *book* that the dreamer is given signifies an invitation to delve deeper into the spiritual heritage and culture of his ancestors.

There is no time here for further exploration into how the nature and development of our dreamer's personality was influenced by this and subsequent imaginations. Suffice it to say that he finally achieved full self-awareness and self-confidence, and that this was clearly reflected in his external life.

---

1. C.G. Jung: *Psychology and Alchemy*. Princeton & London, 1953, CW, Vol. XII, p. 160

Psychologo-Religious Reflections

In conclusion, I would like to make a few more theoretical observations on the Lilith myth.

Whenever the word *myth* has been used in this book, the term – strictly speaking – has only a limited application because the myth in question is not a complete, self-contained one that unfolds like some ancient Greek drama in a set pattern of introduction, development, peripeteia and lysis. What we have here is more like a series of individual *mythologems*, the sum of which nevertheless forms a kind of brightly-colored mosaic, providing us with a reasonably clear and impressive picture of the mythological figure.

The widespread dissemination of the myth of the divine, man-seducing whore on the one hand and the child-killing, life-threatening goddess on the other, together with the primitive traits of the individual mythical motifs, reveal Lilith to be an *archetypal* figure or, more precisely, a specific manifestation of the archetype of the Great Female, which encompasses both the mother and the anima aspect.

But its widespread dissemination failed to save this archaic myth from being gradually watered down over the centuries. For even where it is still alive – in legends and folklore – it still gives us only a hazy picture of the goddess concerned. Jewish mythology is the one exception, in that it has kept the Lilith image vivid to the present day. That is one reason we are now going to consider the problem of how this

image is reflected in the psyche of present-day Jews –
although, over and above that, a universal human
problem is involved: the confrontation with the *dark
aspect* of the feminine.

At the beginning of this book, we established that,
in the course of time, Lilith acquired a markedly
bipolar character. She is both the seductive, enticing
anima and the terrifying *mother.*

However, these two sides to her character are not
always clearly kept apart in mythology. Thus, in the
Gilgamesh epic, Ishtar first appears as an anima figure and then as a terrifying mother who transforms
her lovers into animals. Similarly, in the Zohar, Lilith
appears initially as the seductive anima and later as
the mother who kills her lovers.

The reason for the mixing of these two aspects
seems to me to lie in the fact that they both betray an
archaic attitude of mind, in which the individual
figures are only vaguely defined. In addition, these
individual figures blend into each other. It was only
as a result of the continuing development of consciousness that their outlines became clearer and
differentiated. *Neumann* plainly recognized this process:

> "It is like those pictures which, so long as they are not
> sharply focused, seem to be without contours and ut-
> terly confusing, but which fall into a pattern when the
> observer stands off at the right distance. Figures, mass-
> es, relations now become visible, whereas before they
> had remained blurred and indecipherable. The devel-
> opment of consciousness is more or less analogous to
> this alteration of vision; indeed it seems to be directly
> dependent upon how far consciousness succeeds in
> gaining the distance that will enable it to perceive

distinct forms and meanings, where before was noth-ing but ambiguity and murk."[1]

In the process of development of consciousness, the first phase results in a differentiation between the individual archetypes within the sea of the collec-tive unconscious. Thus, for example, the image of the Great Mother moves into the conscious realm from that of the collective unconscious. A second phase results in the splitting off of certain aspects from the archetype – for example, the anima is split off from the mother archetype. According to *Jung*, this:

> "... in a man's psychology invariably appears, at first, mingled with the mother-image."[2]

In the second phase, there occurs what *Neumann* describes as the release of the anima from the moth-er archetype.[3]

This development occurs both collectively in my-thology – for example, in the myth of the fight with the dragon, in which the mother is overpowered and the anima is "released" – and also in the individual sphere. Here, the anima is mostly projected into a figure which, as mother and lover, embodies both the aspect of the mother and of the anima. Only when one is freed from the clutches of the maternal image can one actually encounter the anima.

In the third phase, the polar opposites are at last visible within an archetype. Thus, for example, the Great Mother is divided into the good, caring, nur-

1. E. Neumann: *loc. cit.*, p. 353f
2. C.G. Jung: "Psychological Aspects of the Mother Archetype" in *The Archetypes and the Collective Unconscious*. Princeton & London, 1959, CW, IX, p. 82
3. E. Neumann: *loc. cit.*

turing mother and the terrifying, devouring mother, or the anima into the seductive anima and the inspirational anima.

As far as the Lilith myth is concerned, the division of the mother is easy to see – although it occurred relatively late.

With regard to the figure of the *mother,* her negative character – the Lamashtû aspect – is so far to the fore that her bright aspect doesn't put in an appearance at all, i.e., psychologically speaking, it remains completely in the unconscious. However, it can be detected without difficulty in other mythical contexts and connections.

In the case of the *anima,* the division into her polar opposites is clearly visible, in that her negative aspect appears in the Ishtar side and the positive in that of Eve and the Shekhinah.

If Lilith really is a figure from the depths of the collective unconscious, i.e., an archetypal figure, then we must assume that she confronts both men and women in both her aspects. This would mean that she also encounters men in the guise of a terrifying mother. The situation with women is different insofar as Lilith is a being of the same sex and thus is more like a shadow figure of the woman concerned. As the analytical experience with Jews shows, this does indeed seem to be the case. In our *myth,* on the other hand, the anima aspect confronts the man and the mother aspect confronts the woman.

Lilith's *anima aspect* does not only show in her attitude towards present-day men but was already apparent in her behavior towards the first man, Adam, who in the myth represented to a certain degree the male prototype. Here, Lilith has all the characteristics typical of anima figures, even though her dark aspect predominates from the outset. She is the shadow beloved of Adam who, drawn by her beauty, simplicity and maybe also by her natural physical attraction and unrestrained wildness, tries to make her his companion. Quite soon, though, she makes a power and superiority claim against him that Adam will not bow to. Indeed, in this case, he *must* not do so, if he doesn't want to risk becoming totally subordinate to her and losing his manhood as a result. The outcome of this power struggle is that Adam and Lilith split up and Lilith disappears. But just as she originally attempted to seduce Adam, she still tries to seduce all men to this very day.

In psychological terms, this purely natural, instinctive anima attempts over and over again to approach a man, i.e., to force her way into a consciousness that she feels should absorb her. Like numerous other anima figures which appear to us in myths, fairy tales and legends, such as the melusines, nymphs, sirens and ondines, Lilith also tries to associate with humans. Only in this way – that is, psychologically speaking, accepted by a receptive, steadfast consciousness, can she be "released," i.e., transformed.

It is these natural beings that, according to *Emma Jung*:

> "... with charms or enchanting songs they (sirens, the Lorelei, and so on) lure a man into their realm, where he disappears forevermore; or else – a very important point – they try to bind a man in the chains of love, that they may live in his world with him."[1]

This means that the encounter between a man and his anima image can have either positive or

1. E. Jung: "The Anima as an Elemental Being" in *Animus and Anima*. New York, 1957, p. 46

tragic consequences. Either the anima is absorbed into the male consciousness and is integrated with it, or the man becomes enslaved by her, which results in his complete possession by the anima and a consequent loss of ego.

However, in our myth, the dark character of Lilith is so much in the foreground that all attempts at forcing a way into the man's consciousness are doomed to failure from the start. In addition, the anima, which according to her inner nature embodies the *eros* principle, cannot in the least be accepted at first by a consciousness that is to a certain extent identified with the *logos* principle.

Everything that occurs *collectively* in the myth is reflected in the *individual* sphere: the appearance of Lilith in the Lilith dream indicates that this aspect of the unconscious should be absorbed by the consciousness. But the figure's markedly baleful character causes the dreamer so many fears and inhibitions that his consciousness is not at all in a position to look at it, let alone to absorb it. Accordingly, the dreamer remains cut off from his anima image and his one-sided male consciousness undergoes no transformation. At the same time, the anima, too, remains fettered and on her purely natural level, thus also undergoing no transformation. In other words, the transformation process, which should include both the consciousness and the unconscious, fails to materialize.

The creatures which result from Adam's temporary association with Lilith are not human but demonic, since she has not yet developed her human side in her relations with him. Lilith, therefore, remains above all a seductive, tempting and dangerous anima figure. This side is also clearly expressed in medieval legends and pictorial representations in which it is not Eve but Lilith, in the form of the serpent in the Garden of Eden, who tempts Adam to eat the apple from the Tree of Knowledge.

Since the man's clear consciousness cannot absorb the dark anima image, there is a provisional interruption of psychic development, because no transformation occurs to either the consciousness or the unconscious. Lilith remains on her instinctive level and the man, when he encounters her, must be careful not to be seized by her – that is, psychologically speaking, not to be possessed by the anima.

Lilith's unsuccessful union with Adam results in her departure either into the desert, to remote spots or ruins, or – together with other ghostly figures and unclean animals – to the Red Sea. In other words, she sinks back into the unconscious from which she had originally emerged.

The more human aspect of the anima is represented in this version of the myth by Eve, who was created from one of Adam's ribs and possesses a human character. The children of this union are, therefore, not demonic but human.

Whereas, in the myth, Lilith offers men almost exclusively her anima side, she always presents women with the aspect of a terrible, death-bringing mother.

At the beginning of the book, it was established that this aspect was connected with – indeed, was to a certain extent shaped by – the image of the terrifying Babylonian mother goddess, Lamashtû. How far such a direct, historically establishable dependence of the Lilith picture on Sumero-Babylonian "models" really went is not of any great importance from the psychological standpoint but is actually an historico-religious problem. Even if one wishes to assume such a dependence, which could only be explained by the migration of the myth, there remains the question of the choice of motif; in other words: why precisely was the image of a child-stealing and child-killing mother goddess or a seductive demonic figure borrowed from Sumero-Babylonian mythology, while many other mythologems of this culture group, whose appropriation was equally as feasible, were left on one side?

The more likely assumption is that this figure clearly touched an unconscious, latent but ever-present universal (i.e., archetypal) image in the Jewish unconscious and perhaps even constellated it. On its "reception" into Jewish mythology – or, psychologically speaking, on its spontaneous emergence – the Lilith image underwent certain transformations. A first transformation occurred, as we have already established, in the biblical-Talmudic tradition, where Lilith, having been an archaic goddess, turned into a colorless night and desert ghost.

However, the second transformation, which took place within Jewish mysticism, is far more deep-reaching. The feature of the Kabbalah which is fundamental to Judaism lies in its very remythologization of Judaism. The result – to use *Scholem*'s striking phrase – is a "revolt of the images." This means that the old images and symbols won back their significance. Lilith regains her original dignity through being absorbed into the realm of the – admittedly dark – Sefiroth and thereby into the pleroma.

As the dark opponent of the Shekhinah, which in the Kabbalistic mythology embodies the positive aspect of the feminine,[1] Lilith represents the negative aspect, which, in the guise of a devouring mother, attempts to destroy the newborn child, the new consciousness or the young self, by drinking its blood, i.e., the carrier of vegetative-animal life. This sharply reveals the whole, dangerous vampire nature of Lilith, who needs the child's life in order to live herself to such an extreme that Lilith, as a later legendary story tells, even murders her own children if she cannot find someone else's children to kill.[2] By so doing, she ends by turning the terrible side of her character against herself.

The question arises as to why precisely *this* myth emerged from the Jewish unconscious and has lasted for thousands of years. The answer is connected with both historical and psychological backgrounds.

It cannot be established with certainty from the available Sumerian and Babylonian texts whether there was ever a cultic worship of Lamashtû. All that can be said is that the ancient Babylonian magic and invocation texts do allow for such a possibility. In ancient Israel, however, there is no talk of a cult of Lilith, although the Shedim and Se'irim referred to with Lilith enjoyed cultic worship for many years. But in the course of the Deuteronomic *cult reform* under King Josiah, around 600 B.C. at the latest, all cults of foreign gods and demons were definitively eliminated. Perhaps this formed the point of departure for that specific development which finally led to the shaping of an emphatically patriarchal and spiritual image of God which was continued in Talmudic-

---

1. In other mythical references, the Shekhinah can appear ambivalent or negatively destructive, as can Eve
2. Midrash Num. rabba XVI 19

Rabbinic Judaism. On the other hand, it also brought about a real *demythologization* of Judaism, of which the imagelessness of the YHWH cult is but one example. Moreover, this particular developmental tendency has serious psychological consequences – for along with Josiah's cult reforms came first a devaluation and finally a suppression of the Canaanitic gods and, above all, of their chthonic *mother deities.* Thus, the once divine Shedim and Se'irim, together with Lilith, became mere shadowy demons and night spirits, which generally lived in the desert, i.e., in a place which, for the Jewish consciousness of that time, symbolized either their place of origin or, equally, all that was sinister, unknown and dangerous; in other words, the unconscious. The same thing happened with the Canaanitic gods of Baal and the female Asherot. In the end, the practice was taken to such an extreme that the name Shed or demon became synonymous with the epithet for all heathen gods.[1]

Now, one may wonder whether the Lilith myth represents a *regression* into earlier paganism. If regression is taken to mean a return to an earlier state of consciousness, then, indeed, one cannot actually rule out regressive tendencies in Old Testament Judaism, of which both the Books of the Kings and the Prophets can provide more than enough examples. Thus, *Ezekiel*[2] refers to the women weeping for Tammuz at the north gate of the Temple in Jerusalem, and *Jeremiah*[3] predicts disaster for the people who offer sacrifices to the queen of heaven, Ishtar, and

1. H.L. Strack & P. Billerbeck: "Kommentar zum Neuen Testament" in *Talmud und Midrasch.* Munich, 1928, Vol. IV, 1, p. 501
2. Ezek.: 8, 14
3. Jer.: 44, 17

pour out drink offerings to her. The *Second Book of Kings*[1] even speaks of the setting up of a statue of Ishtar or Ashera in the Temple in Jerusalem.

However, as far as Lilith is concerned, it seems to me that the circumstances are different. In this case, it would be incorrect to speak of a regression. There are far more grounds for considering Lilith as the embodiment of a bit of pre-Yahwistic paganism which, in this guise, could not be integrated into the Jewish consciousness of the time. Such *relics* of religious history from earlier stages of development are, incidentally, not difficult to detect in the comparative history of religion and mythological research. Thus, one can say – to give just two examples – that Kundry in Wolfram von Eschenbach's "Parzival" and the Lady Venus in the folk song about Tannhäuser correspond to heathen relics, which could not be integrated into the Christian consciousness of the day.

That is why these figures were driven out of the consciousness and acquired a demonic character in consequence. A real process of suppression took place whereby they were pushed away into the unconscious, where they wander around like ghosts and their unholy activities multiply – for experience shows that such figures, when expelled, become not only autonomous but also highly destructive.

Incidentally, the consequences for the above-mentioned process of demythologization for biblical and Talmudic-Rabbinic Judaism can be pursued into the psychology of modern *Jews. Neumann* put his finger on this when he pointed out that:

1. II Kings 31, 7

"The world of the Old Testament is very much colored by this revaluation in which all the maternal-chthonic characteristics of the primitive world of the Canaanites were devalued, reinterpreted, and replaced by a patriarchal Jehovah-valuation. This Jehovah-earth polarity is a basic factor in Jewish psychology, and unless it is understood it is not possible to understand the Jews."[1]

I would like to suggest a certain qualification of this rather generalized thesis. The psychology of contemporary Jews is certainly not characterized exclusively by biblical-Rabbinic tradition. Its unconscious side is just as much shaped by the Kabbalah. Here, the whole significance of Jewish mysticism, with its rich, mythological world of imagery, reveals itself. Here, the feminine takes its rightful place once more and regains its due rank.

In addition, one important fact should not be overlooked. The development and differentiation of the Western, Judaeo-Christian consciousness *had to* lead first to a certain repression of the feminine at that time, as *Neumann* rightly stresses:

"The supersession of the matriarchal by a patriarchal epoch is an archetypal process; that is to say, it is a universal and necessary phenomenon in the history of mankind."[2]

Precisely this archetypical character of development shows the need to surmount the originally more matriarchally-formed degree of consciousness by a patriarchal and spiritual further development.

The fact that this development was *universal* and *necessary* is frequently ignored today, in the age of

1. E. Neumann: *loc. cit.*, p. 433, note
2. E. Neumann: *The Origins and History of Consciousness.* Princeton, 1954, p. 245

women's struggle for emancipation. Indeed, it has even become the fashion virtually to condemn patriarchy and hold it responsible for all the abortive attempts in the development of Western consciousness. *H. Wolff*,[1] among others, did not escape this temptation, when she painted the patriarchy at the time of Christ in the blackest of colors. In contrast, *Rivkah Kluger-Schärf* quite rightly states:

> "As a result of the obvious dark sides of patriarchal thinking, a tendency has grown up in the present day to devalue patriarchy and idealize matriarchy. But one should not forget that the dark sides of matriarchal origins are chaos, an indistinct swamp, which yearns for redemption, an eternal cycle of death and birth from which no development would have arisen without the emergence of a new, spiritual principle. The desirable goal, as it appears in myths, legends and dreams, is not a 'mother world' as opposed to a 'father world' but the union of feminine and masculine."[2]

A certain balance between an exclusively masculine and feminine attitude is given us by Jewish mysticism. The Lilith motif, as it has developed within that mysticism, strikes me as somewhat of a compensation – together with the equivalent Shekhinah myth – for the one-sided spiritual-patriarchal conscious attitude.

In this, the collective consciousness identifies itself to some degree with a divine image, to which correspond the symbols of spirit, father and heaven. In contrast, Lilith represents an aspect of the unconscious which was devalued by the dominant collec-

---

1. H. Wolff: *Jesus der Mann. Die Gestalt Jesu in tiefenpsychologischer Sicht.* Stuttgart, 1975, p. 126ff
2. R. Kluger-Schärf: *Psyche and Bible.* New York, 1974, p. 130

tive attitude. To her are assigned the symbols of nature, mother and earth. In the process, the first cycle of symbols is valued by the dominant patriarchal consciousness as predominantly bright and positive, whereas the second is considered to be dark and negative. A new orientation in Jewish values only developed in Kabbalistic mythology. There, a division of the feminine into its opposites takes place: the dark Lilith faces the bright Shekhinah.

According to her original nature, Lilith is an archaic goddess. Psychologically speaking, this means that she *possesses a spiritual reality, she is just as real an inner factor as an external figure would be.* Her aspect as a terrible mother places her in the group of universally distributed *underworld and death goddesses,* like Kali in India, Gorgo in early Greek mythology, the Aztecs' Tlamatecuhtli, Chicomecoatl in Mexico, Hel-Holda in the Germanic myth and Le-hev-hev in Melanesia.

In her *anima* aspect, too, she has numerous parallels, like Aphrodite, Artemis, Lorelei and the many other figures of Greek, Roman and Germanic mythology.

If the Lilith myth is an actual living myth, then the question arises as to what this symbol means for a contemporary person and how he or she relates to this internal figure. In other words, what does the confrontation with the dark aspect of the feminine mean to people today? Since an archetypal figure is involved, most people, insofar as they undergo a development and modification of consciousness, come into contact in some way or other with the problem of the feminine in its negative aspect. The difficulties which arise from an encounter with this particular side are different, depending on whether a man or a woman is involved.

For a man living in a predominantly patriarchal culture, there are very specific problems. Because patriarchy dominates in the development of the Judaeo-Christian-Western history of ideas, a man trapped in this particular culture has difficulties in resolving his anima problem. As a result, most men might prefer to avoid this thorny problem and suppress it, as long as internal or external need does not force them to confront it. Another possibility is to intellectualize the problem and put it into words, without experiencing it emotionally in one's innermost depths. This means that the man generally prefers – insofar as he is intellectually capable – to suppress his behavioral and emotional problems and to remain unconscious of them.

Such a defensive attitude is psychologically comprehensible to a certain extent, because a confrontation with the anima carries with it all kinds of dangers for a man, as the myths and legends of all races clearly indicate: to acquire the treasure or free the anima, one must first overcome the terrible mother.

For a man, I see a danger in a confrontation with the anima when, as in the Lilith myth, it comes to a power struggle. In this struggle, he runs the risk of defeat, with the result that his manliness could be damaged. If he persists because of his claim to male superiority, the danger arises that he will be cut off both from his eros and his emotions. Between these two possibilities lies only a narrow path that the self-aware man must follow if he wants to integrate his anima and still retain his manliness.

Lewandowski[1] supports the view that an encounter with Lilith presents a greater threat to a man than to a woman. She puts this down to the fact that men are generally physically weaker than women. This explanation might appear illuminating at first sight, but in my opinion it is not completely satisfactory from a psychological point of view. I am of a contrary opinion: that the encounter with Lilith carries greater dangers for a woman than for a man. This might possibly be connected with the fact that the anima is more adaptable than the terrible mother. *Neumann* has already referred to this aspect:

> "The anima figure, despite the great danger that is bound up with it, is not terrible in the same way as the Great Mother, who is not at all concerned with the independence of the individual and the ego. Even when the anima is seemingly negative and 'intends,' for example, to poison the male consciousness, to endanger it by intoxication, and so on – even then a positive reversal is possible, for the anima figure is always subject to defeat."[2]

The confrontation with the dark, feminine side, which approaches a man either externally as a woman or internally as an anima, but which approaches a woman externally as a shadow figure or internally as her own self-destructive forces, signifies a unique opportunity for a man: depending on how he stands up to this conflict, he is given a chance to develop his consciousness. However, this does not only involve a change to his one-sided masculine consciousness,

1. A. Lewandowski: *loc. cit.*, p. 85
2. E. Neumann: *The Great Mother.* Princeton & London, 1955, p. 35

but also – happily – a similar alteration to previously negative internal figures.

One might ask oneself whether it is primarily the appearance of the anima image or – viewed from the outside – of the woman which brings about this change, or whether the dreams and imaginations cause it. Probably, it is a case of parallel processes of development. *Jung*[1] posed this question in connection with the transformation of the divine image, but left the answer to it open. In his work "The Psychology of the Transference," he referred to the various stages of the anima:

> "Four stages of eroticism were known in the late classical period: Hawwah (Eve), Helen (of Troy), the Virgin Mary, and Sophia. The series is repeated in Goethe's Faust: in the figures of Gretchen as the personification of a purely instinctual relationship (Eve); Helen as an anima figure; Mary as the personification of the 'heavenly,' i.e., Christian or religious, relationship; and the 'eternal feminine' as an expression of the alchemical Sapientia. As the nomenclature shows, we are dealing with the heterosexual Eros, or anima-figure in four stages, and consequently with four stages of the Eros cult. The first stage – Hawwah, Eve, earth – is purely biological; woman is equated with the mother and only represents something to be fertilized. The second stage is still dominated by the sexual Eros, but on an aesthetic and romantic level where woman has already acquired some value as an individual. The third stage raises Eros to the heights of religious devotion and thus spiritualizes him: Hawwah has been replaced by

1. C.G. Jung: *Aion. Researches into the Phenomenology of the Self.* Princeton & London, 1959, CW, Vol. IX, 2, p. 202ff
   S. Hurwitz: "Die Gestalt des sterbenden Messias" in *Studienreihe aus dem C.G. Jung Institut, Zürich.* Vol. VIII. Zurich, 1958, p. 218f

spiritual motherhood. Finally, the fourth stage illustrates something which unexpectedly goes beyond the almost unsurpassable third stage: Sapientia. How can wisdom transcend the most holy and the most pure? – Presumably only by virtue of the truth that the less sometimes means the more. This stage represents a spiritualization of Helen and consequently of Eros as such."[1]

Perhaps one can consider the female figures, Lilith, Eve and the Shekhinah, which appear in the Lilith myth, as three stages of the anima, in which the Shekhinah corresponds to Sophia and sapientia.

That the figure of Mary is missing in our myth may be explained by the structural differences between the Jewish and the Christian attitude. Judaism cannot accept Mary with her one-sided spirituality or Christ with his overemphasized bright side.

Let us, in conclusion, return to our dreamer. It must be said that the encounter with the dark side of the internal anima and of the external Lilith-like woman required of the dreamer a great deal of patience, tenacity, stamina and, above all, trust in the helpful powers of the unconscious. But precisely this experience of the grandeur of the unconscious led more and more to an internal strengthening and discovery of his own identity. His readiness to take his anima problem seriously and to subject himself willingly to the peripeteia of the process of development and maturity led to a transformation that affected both his consciousness and his unconscious.

An encounter between the masculine consciousness and the unconscious gives rise to various possi-

---

1. C.G. Jung: "The Psychology of the Transference" in *The Practice of Psychotherapy*. Princeton & London, 1954, CW, Vol. XVI, p. 174

bilities, one of which is of a bright anima image confronting the dark anima image, as, for example, in the Shekhinah confronting Lilith. However, the possibility also arises that the dark feminine itself begins to change and gradually assumes a positive shape, as is shown by the example of the active imagination. This transformation of the internal image is already evident in connection with the Lilith dream, in that, in the course of the active imagination, the black Lilith anima first moved from the left to the right side. Gradually, an internal dialogue began. The internal discussion with her often took on a highly dramatic character. But at the same time, she began visibly to lose her blackness, savagery and compulsiveness and, with them, her primitive character, until in the final encounter she appeared as a human being, the maiden Simcha-Lilith.

Such a transformation of the dark side of the feminine can be traced in the collective sphere, too, notably in other myths. One example of this is the Mandaean myth, with its transformation of the Lilith image, which gains greater prominence from its elevation to the realm of light – in other words, as a result of an increasing dawning of consciousness. Another possibility is to be found in the Shekhinah mysticism of the Kabbalists. Here, Lilith, the "mother of all demons," confronts the Shekhinah, the "mother of Israel."

Just as in the Lilith myth the two opposing anima aspects are embodied in Lilith and Eve, so in the Kabbalah they appear to us as the opposing chthonic and spiritual mothers. The conscious experience and acceptance of these two opposing aspects of the feminine contains a possibility of their integration, which could lead to a further development of consciousness in the sense of a *process of self-realization.* However, whether in the end a man is internally ready to follow this path is on the one hand a question of his personal fate, and on the other of his responsibility for his life's work: his *individuation.*

Bibliography

Albright, W.F.: "An Aramaean Text in Hebrew from the seventh Century B.C." in BASOR, New Haven, 1939

Alphabeta de'ben Sira: ed. M. Steinschneider, Berlin, 1858

Baer, Y.: *A History of Jews in Christian Spain.* Philadelphia, 1961, Vol. I

Baron, S.W.: *A Social and Religious History of the Jews.* Philadelphia, 1958, Vol. II

Begg, E.: "From Lilith to Lourdes" in *Journal of Analytical Psychology*, London, 1983

Beyer, R.: *Die Königin von Saba. Engel und Dämon. Der Mythos einer Frau.* Bergisch Gladbach, 1987

Black-Koltuv, B.: *The Book of Lilith.* York Beach, 1986

Blau, L.: *Das altjüdische Zauberwesen.* Budapest, 1898

Bonner, C.: *Studies in Magical Amulets chiefly Graeco-Egyptian.* Ann Arbor, 1950

Brandt, W.: *Die mandäische Religion, ihre Entwicklung und geschichtliche Bedeutung.* Utrecht, 1899

Buren, E.D. van: "A further note on the Terra-cotta Relief" in AfO, Berlin, 1936/37, Vol. XI

— "An Enlargement of a Given Theme" in OR, Rome, 1951, Vol. XX

— *Clay Figurines from Babylonia and Assyria.* London, 1930, Figs. 130 & 131

Caquot, A. & du Mesnil du Buisson:"La seconde Tablette ou 'petite Amulette' d'Arslan Tash" in *Syrie.* Paris, 1971, Vol. XXXXVIII

Charles, R.H.: *The Apocrypha and Pseudepigrapha of the Old Testament.* London, 1913, Vol. II

Cohn, M.: JL, Berlin, 1928, Vol. II

Contenau, G.: *La Magie chez les Assyriens et les Bayloniens.* Paris, 1947

Cross, F.M. & Saley, R.J.: "Phoenician Incantations on a Plaque of the Seventh Century B.C. from Arslan Tash in Upper Syria" in BASOR, New Haven, 1970

Dan, Y.: "Alphabeta de'ben Sira" in EJ, Jerusalem, 1972, Vol. VII

Daum, W.: *Die Königin von Saba. Kunst, Legende und Archäologie zwischen Morgenland und Abendland.* Zurich & Stuttgart, 1988

Desmoulins, J. & Ambelain, R.: *Elements d'Astrologie scientifique. Lilith le second satellite de la terre.* Paris, n.d.

Donner, H. & Röllig, W.: *Kanaanäische und aramäische Inschriften.* Wiesbaden, 1966

Dow, R.P.: "Studies in the Old Testament" in BBES, Brooklyn, 1917, Vol. XII

Drescher, J.: "A Coptic Amulet" in *Coptic Studies* in honor of W.E. Crum. Boston, 1950

Drower, E.S.: MII, London, 1937

— *The Canonical Prayerbook of the Mandaeans.* Leiden, 1959

du Mesnil du Buisson: "Une Tablette magique de la Région du Moyen Euphrate" in *Mélanges syriens offerts à René Dussaud.* Paris, 1939, Vol. I

Duhm, H.: *Die bösen Geister im Alten Testament.* Tübingen & Leipzig, 1904

Dupont-Sommer, A.: "Deux Lamelles d'Argent à l'Inscription Hébréo-Araméenne trouvées à Agabeyli" in JKF, Heidelberg, 1950/51, Vol. I

—	"L'Inscription de l'amulette d'Arslan Tash" in RHR, Paris, 1939, Vol. CXX
Ebeling, E.:	*Keilinschriften aus Assur religiösen Inhalts.* Leipzig, 1922
—	*Tod und Leben nach den Vorstellungen der Babylonier.* Berlin & Leipzig, 1931
Epstein, J.N.:	"Glosses Babylo-Araméennes" in REJ, Paris, 1921, Vol. LXXIII & MAIT, 1922, Vol. LXXIV
Fankhauser, A.:	*Das wahre Gesicht der Astrologie.* Zurich, 1932
Fischer-Homberger, E.:	*Hypochondrie.* Bern, Stuttgart & Wien, 1970
Foerster, W.:	*The Hypostasis of the Archons in Gnosis. A Selection of Gnostic Texts.* Oxford, 1972, Vol. I
Fontenrose, J.:	Python. *A Study of Delphic Myth and its Origin.* Berkeley & Los Angeles, 1959
Fossey, C.:	*La Magie assyrienne.* Paris, 1902
Frank, C.:	"Lamastû, Pazuzû und andere Dämonen. Ein Beitrag zur babylonisch-assyrischen Dämonologie" in MAG, Leipzig, 1941, Vol. XIV, No. 2
Frankfort, H.:	"The Burney Relief" in AfO, Berlin, 1937/39, Vol. XII
Franz, M.-L. von:	"The Dream of Descartes" in *Dreams.* Boston, 1991
—	"Die aktive Imagination in der Psychologie C.G. Jungs" in W. Bitter: *Meditation in Religion und Psychotherapie.* Stuttgart, 1958
—	*The Passion of Perpetua.* Irving, 1980
—	*Die Visionen des Niklaus von Flüe.* Zurich, 1980, 1991
—	*An Introduction to the Psychology of Fairy Tales.* Zurich / New York, 1975
—	*Psychotherapy.* Boston, 1993

Freud, S.:   *Mourning and Melancholia.* London,
                    1957, Standard Edition, Vol. 14

—   *A General Introduction to Psychoanalysis,*
                    Transl. Joan Riviere. New York, 1920

Furlani, G.:   "Il Nomine dei Classi dei Demoni
                    presso i Mandei" in RANL, Rome, 1954,
                    Vol. IX

Gaster, M.:   "Two thousand years of a charm against
                    the childstealing witch" in *Studies and
                    Texts in Folklore, Magic, Mediaeval
                    Romance, Hebrew Apocrypha and
                    Samaritan Archaeology.* New York, 1971

Gaster, T.H.:   "A Canaanitic Magical Text" in OR,
                    Rome, 1942, Vol. XI

—   "A Hang-Up for Hang-Ups. The second
                    Amuletic Plaque from Arslan Tash" in
                    BASOR, New Haven, 1973

—   "The Child-stealing witch among the
                    Hittites" in SMSR, Bologna, 1952, Vol.
                    XXIII

—   *Myth, Legend and Custom in the Old
                    Testament.* New York & Evanston, 1969

Gollancz, H.:   The Book of Protection being a
                    Collection of Charms, now edited for
                    the first time from Syria. MSS. London
                    1912 & 84

Gordon, C.H.:   "An Aramaic Exorcism" in AO, Prague,
                    1934, Vol. VI

—   "Aramaic Incantation Bowls" in OR,
                    Rome, 1941, Vol. X

—   "Two Magical Bowls in Teheran" in OR,
                    Rome, 1951, Vol. XX

—   Aramaic and Mandaic Bowls in AO,
                    Prague, 1937, Vol. IX (Text L)

Grasowski, J.:   *Milon shimushi le'sapha ha'ivrith.* Tel
                    Aviv, 1937

Gravelaine, J. de & Aimé, J.: *Lilith dans L'Astrologie*. Paris, 1974

Gray, J: *Mythologie des Nahen Ostens*. Wiesbaden, 1969

Grünwald, M.:   MGJV, Hamburg, 1898, No. 5

Heller, B.:   "Das Alphabet des ben Sira" in EJ, Berlin, 1928, Vol. II

Heyer, G.R.:   *Dürers Melancholie und ihre Symbolik*. Zurich, 1935

Horney, K.:   "Die Angst vor der Frau" in *Internationale Zeitschrift für Psychoanalyse*. Vienna, 1932, Vol. XVIII

Hurwitz, S.:   "Die Gestalt des sterbenden Messias" in *Studienreihe aus dem C.G. Jung Institut, Zürich*. Vol. VIII. Zurich, 1958

—   "Sabbatai Zvi" in *Psyche und Erlösung*. Zurich, 1983

—   *The God Image in the Kabbala*. New York, 1954

Jacobsen, T.H.:   *The Sumerian King List*. Chicago, 1939

Jaffé, A.:   "Bilder und Symbole aus E.T.A. Hofmanns Märchen 'Der Goldne Topf'" in C.G. Jung: *Gestalten des Unbewußten*. Zurich, 1950; as separate book: Einsiedeln, 1990

Jean, J.F.:   *Le péché chez les Bayloniens et Assyriens*. Paris, 1925

Jenik, A.:   *Lilith – der schwarze Mond*. Berlin, 1930

Jung, C.G.:   "A Psychological Approach to the Dogma of the Trinity" in *Psychology & Religion: West & East*. Princeton & London, 1958, CW, Vol. XI

—   *Aion. Researches into the Phenomenology of the Self*. Princeton & London, 1959, CW, Vol. IX, 2

—   Letter to James Kirsch in *Letters of C.G. Jung*. Princeton & London, 1972, Vol. II

—   *Psychologische Interpretation von Kinderträumen und älterer Literatur über Träume.* Zurich, 1938/39

—   *Psychology and Alchemy.* Princeton & London, 1953, CW, Vol. XII

—   *The Archetypes and the Collective Unconscious.* Princeton & London, 1959, CW, Vol. IX

—   *The Practice of Psychotherapy.* Princeton & London, CW, 1954, Vol. XVI

—   *The Transcendent Function.* Princeton & London, 1960, CW, Vol. VIII

—   *Two Essays on Analytical Psychology.* Princeton & London, 1953, CW, Vol. VII

—   "The Tavistock Lectures" (1935), in *The Symbolic Life*, CW Vol. XVIII, Princeton & London, 1976

Jung, E.:   "The Anima as an Elemental Being" in *Animus and Anima.* New York, 1957

K. Kerényi: *The Gods of the Greeks.* London and New York, 1951

Killen, A.M.:   "La Légende de Lilith" in ALC, Paris, 1932, Vol. XII

Kluger-Schärf, R.: *Psyche and Bible.* New York, 1974

Kohut, A.:   *Über die jüdische Angelologie und Dämonologie in ihrer Abhängigkeit vom Parsismus.* Leipzig, 1866, par. 86

Kraeling, E.G.:   "A unique Babylonian Relief" in BASOR, New Haven, 1937

Kramer, S.N.:   "Gilgamesh and the Huluppu-Tree. A Reconstructed Sumerian Text" in *Assyriological Studies of the Oriental Institute of the University of Chicago.* Chicago, 1938

Krause, M. & Labib, P.: "Die drei Versionen des Apokryphon des Johannes" in *Abhandlungen des Deutschen Archäologischen Instituts Kairo*. Wiesbaden, 1962, Vol. I

Kristianpoller, A.: "Gottesnamen in Talmud und Midrasch" in JL, Vol. II

Langdon, S.H.: "Babylonian and Hebrew Demonology with reference to the supposed borrowing of Persian Dualism in Judaism and Christianity" in IRAS, London, 1934

— "Semitic Mythology" in *The Mythology of all Races*. Boston, 1931, Vol. V

— *Tammuz und Ischtar*. Oxford, 1914.

Layard, A.H.: *Discoveries in the Ruins of Niniveh and Babylon*. London, 1853

Leisegang, H.: *Die Gnosis*. Leipzig, 1924

Lenherr-Baumgartner, C.: *Lilith-Eva*. Zurich, 1986

Lenormant, F.: *La Magie chez les Chaldéens et les origines accadiennes*. Paris, 1874

Lewandowski, A.: *The God-Image, Source of Evil*. Zurich, 1977

Lévi, I.: "Lilit et Lilin" in REJ, Paris, 1914, Vol. LXXVIII

Lidzbarski, M.: "Das Qolasta" in ML, Berlin, 1920

— GR, Göttingen & Leipzig, 1925

Lutz, H.F.: *Selected Sumerian and Babylonian Texts*. Philadelphia, 1919

McCown, C.C.: *Testamentum Salomonis*. Leipzig, 1922

Meissner, B.: "Neue Siegelcylinder mit Krankheitsbeschwörungen" in AfO, Berlin, 1935/36, Vol. X

— *Babylonien und Assyrien*. Heidelberg, 1920, Vol. I

Montgomery, J.A.: "Some early Amulets from Palestine" in JAOS, New Haven, 1911, Vol. XXXI

—   ARIT, Philadelphia, 1913

Myhrman, D.W.: "Die Labartû-Texte. Babylonische Beschwörungsformeln nebst Zauberverfahren gegen die Dämonin Labartû" in ZA, Strasbourg, 1902, Vol. XVI

Neumann, E.: "Die Angst vor dem Weiblichen" in *Die Angst. Studien aus dem C.G. Jung Institut, Zürich.* Zurich, 1958/59, Vol. X

— "Die mythische Welt und der Einzelne" in *Kulturentwicklung und Religion.* Zurich, 1953

— *The Great Mother.* Princeton & London, 1955

— *The Origin & History of Consciousness.* Princeton & London, 1954

Nordström, F.: *Goya, Saturn and Melancholy.* Uppsala, 1962

Opitz, D.: "Die Probleme des Burney Reliefs" in AfO, Berlin, 1937/39, Vol. XII

— "Die vogelfüssige Göttin auf den Löwen" in AfO, Berlin, 1936/37, Vol. XI

Panofsky, E. & Saxl, F.: "Dürers Melencolia I" in *Studien der Bibliothek Warburg.* Leipzig & Berlin, 1923, Vol. II

Patai, R.: *The Hebrew Goddess.* Forest Hills, 1967

Perera, S.B.: *Descent to the Goddess: A Way of Initiation for Women.* Toronto, 1981

Perles, F.: "Noch einmal Labartû im Alten Testament" in OLZ, Leipzig, 1915, Vol. XVIII

Petroff, J.: JE, Jerusalem 1971, Vol. XV

Plaskow Goldenberg, J.: "The Coming of Lilith" in *Religion and Sexism.* Brattleboro, 1974

Pradel, F.: *Griechische und süditalienische Gebete, Beschwörungen und Rezepte des Mittelalters.* Giessen, 1907

Qimchi, D.:   REDAQ to Isa. 34, 14

Quispel, G.:   Book review of W. Foerster: Gnosis. A
                Selection of Gnostic Texts, Vol. II in
                Bibliotheca Orientalis, Leiden, 1975,
                Vol. XXXII Nr. 5/6

—   *Gnosis als Weltreligion.* Zurich, 1951

Ranke Graves, R. von & Patai, R.: *Hebräische Mythologie.*
                Reinbek bei Hamburg, 1986

Rawlinson, H.C.: *Cuneiform Inscriptions of Western Asia.*
                London, 1861/84, V 51

Reitzenstein, R.: *Poimandres. Studien zur griechisch-
                ägyptischen und frühchristlichen Literatur.*
                Leipzig, 1904

Riemschneider, M.: *Die Welt der Hettiter.* Stuttgart 1954

Röllig, W.:   "Die Amulette von Arslan Tash" in *Neue
                Ephemeris für Semitische Epigraphik.*
                Wiesbaden, 1974

Rudolph, K.:   *Die Mandäer.* Göttingen, 1961, Vol. II

—   *Gnosis und Gnostizismus.* Darmstadt,
                1975

Rudwin, M.:   *The Devil in Legend and Literature.*
                Chicago & London, 1931

Sälzle, K.:   *Tier und Mensch, Gottheit und Dämon.*
                Munich, 1965

Scheftelowitz, I.: *Die altpersische Religion und das Judentum.*
                Giessen, 1920

Schmidt, B.:   *Das Volksleben der Neugriechen und das
                hellenische Altertum.* Leipzig, 1871

Scholem, G.:   "A New Interpretation of an Aramaic
                Inscription" in JG, Philadelphia, 1965

—   "Relationship between Gnostic and
                Jewish Sources" in JG, Philadelphia,
                1965

—   "Schechina. Das weiblich-passive Mo-
                ment in der Gottheit" in *Von der mysti-
                schen Gestalt der Gottheit.* Zurich, 1962

—   "Tradition und Neuschöpfung im Ritus der Kabbalisten" in *Zur Kabbala und ihrer Symbolik*. Zurich, 1960

—   *Art. Lilith in Kabbalah*. Jerusalem, 1974

—   *Die jüdische Mystik in ihren Hauptströmungen*. Zurich, 1957

—   JE, Jerusalem 1972, Vol. XI

—   Lilith u'malkat Sheva in Peraqim chadashim me'injenei Ashmedai ve'Lilith. TZ, Jerusalem 1947/48, Vol. XIX

—   *Ursprung und Anfänge der Kabbala*. Berlin, 1962

Schott, A. & Soden, W.v. : *Das Gilgamesch-Epos*. Stuttgart, 1958 (table 6)

Schrader, E.: *Die Keilinschriften und das Alte Testament* ed. H. Zimmern. Berlin, 1902/03

Schrire, T.: *Hebrew Amulets. Their Decipherment and Interpretation*. London, 1966

Shoshan, A. ibn: *Milon chadash*. Jerusalem, 1958

Skeat, W.W.: *Malay Magic*. London, 1900

Strack, H.L. & Billerbeck, P.: "Kommentar zum Neuen Testament" in *Talmud und Midrasch*. Munich, 1928, Vol. IV, 1

Thimme, J.: "Phönizische Elfenbeine in Karlsruhe" in *Antike Welt. Zeitschrift für Archäologie und Urgeschichte*. Feldmeilen, 1973, Vol IV

Thompson, R.C.: *Semitic Magic, its Origin and Development*. London, 1908

—   *The Devils and Evil Spirits in Babylonia*. London, 1903

Thureau-Dangin, F.: "Rituel et amulettes contre Labartu" in RA, Paris, 1921, Vol. XVIII

Torczyner, H.: "A Hebrew Incantation against Night-Demons from Biblical Times" in JHES, Chicago, 1947, Vol. VI

Trachtenberg, J.: *Jewish Magic and Superstition*. New York, 1939

Ungnad, A.:   *Die Religion der Babylonier und Assyrer.* Jena, 1921

Vogelsang, E.W.: *To Redeem the Demonic.* Zurich, 1981

Winkler, H.A.:   *Salomo und die Karina. Eine orientalische Legende von der Bezwingung einer Kindbettdämonin durch einen heiligen Helden.* Stuttgart, 1931

Wittekind, W.:   *Das Hohe Lied und seine Beziehungen zum Ischtarkult.* Hanover, 1925

Wolff, H.:   *Jesus der Mann. Die Gestalt Jesu in tiefenpsychologischer Sicht.* Stuttgart, 1975

Yamauchi, E.M.: "Aramaic Magic Bowls" in JAOS, New Haven, 1965, Vol. LXXXV

—   MAIT in American Oriental Series. New Haven, 1967, Vol. II

Zoller, I.:   "Lilith" in RdA, Rome, 1926

Zunz, L.:   *Die gottesdienstlichen Vorträge der Juden.* Berlin, 1832

Index of Authors

Subject Index

Tess Castleman

Sacred Dream Circles

A Guide to Facilitating Jungian Dream Groups

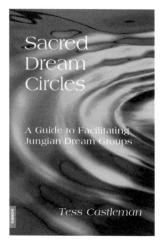

This is a handbook about participating in group dream modalities. Practical exercises included in each chapter anchor the step-by-step instructions given for running a safe, yet deep and meaningful group process with or without a professional facilitator.

Care is taken to discuss shadow projection, clear communication, and confidentiality issues. Topics include: nightmares, recurring dreams, childhood dreams, and synchronicity. Creating the tribal dream, where participants interweave their dream material in a complex yet boundary-safe fabric is the quintessential goal of this companion volume to the author's previous book, *Threads, Knots, Tapestries.*
224 pages, ISBN 978-3-85630-731-8

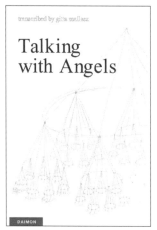

Gitta Mallasz

Talking with Angels

Budaliget 1943: A small village on the edge of Budapest. Three young women and a man, artists and close friends are gathered together in the uneasy days before Hitler's armies would destroy the world as they knew it. Seeking spiritual knowledge, and anticipating the horrors of Nazi-occupied Hungary, they met regularly to discuss how to find their own inner paths to enlightenment. One June afternoon, the meeting is disrupted when Hanna calls out, "Be careful, it is no longer I who speak!" Her friends do not recognize her voice now or later, when she speaks in other voices, each directing a specific message to one of the four.

For 17 months, with the world locked in a deadly struggle for survival, the four friends meet every week with the spiritual beings they come to call their "angels"; Gitta Mallasz takes notes, the protocols which form this book, along with her commentary. The angels' message of personal responsibility is as meaningful and as urgent today as it was for its initial recipients half a century ago.
474 pages, new revised edition, ISBN 978-3-85630-704-2

Eva Wertenschlag-Birkhäuser

Windows on Eternity

The Paintings of Peter Birkhäuser

Peter Birkhäuser's paintings frequently give form to overwhelming contents from the collective unconscious whose sense only becomes apparent when seen in the context of the spiritual predicament of our times. Birkhäuser was uniquely sensitive to the subliminal issues of the age. His whole career demonstrated that his special calling as an artist was to dedicate his abilities to a greater creative spirit and use his art to reveal, not only the crisis and infirmity of our times, but more importantly the reactions and healing impulses of the autonomous psyche. His pictures act as mirrors of the soul, where things hidden within us and our age become visible. In the major themes of the paintings we can observe something resembling a collective process of individuation. This is religious art, a manifestation of an image of God originating in the unconscious, striving to become real as part of a new consciousness. The artist's own personal individuation process becomes a gestation in paintings that circumscribe the birth of a new myth.

200 pages, hardbound, with 53 color plates, ISBN 978-3-85630-715-8

Ann Belford Ulanov

The Wisdom of the Psyche

This book promotes a strong argument for a 'feminine' approach to religious discovery: to struggle in the ambiguous gap between the wisdom of the psyche and the wisdom of Scripture, between our interior experience of God and the exterior reality of God.

The Wisdom of the Psyche urges clergy to help parishioners bring forth their unconscious feelings and images to join their conscious thoughts. In this way, the church allows its members the space to present themselves fully to God and to be fully present to the human need around them.

144 pages, ISBN 978-3-85630-598-7

English Titles from Daimon

English Titles from Daimon

Laurens van der Post - *The Rock Rabbit and the Rainbow*
Jane Reid - *Jung, My Mother and I: The Analytic Diaries
of Catharine Rush Cabot*
R.M. Rilke - *Duino Elegies*
A. Schweizer / R. Schweizer-Vüllers - *Stone by Stone: Reflections on Jung
- Wisdom has Built her House*
Miguel Serrano - *C.G. Jung and Hermann Hesse*
Helene Shulman - *Living at the Edge of Chaos*
D. Slattery / G. Slater (Eds.) - *Varieties of Mythic Experience*
David Tacey - *Edge of the Sacred: Jung, Psyche, Earth*
Susan Tiberghien - *Looking for Gold*
Ann Ulanov - *Spiritual Aspects of Clinical Work*
- *The Female Ancestors of Christ*
- *Healing Imagination*
- *Picturing God*
- *Receiving Woman*
- *Spirit in Jung*
- *The Wisdom of the Psyche*
- *The Wizards' Gate, Picturing Consciousness*
- *The Psychoid, Soul and Psyche*
- *Knots and their Untying*
Ann & Barry Ulanov - *Cinderella and her Sisters*
Eva Wertenschlag-Birkhäuser - *Windows on Eternity:
The Paintings of Peter Birkhäuser*
Harry Wilmer - *How Dreams Help*
- *Quest for Silence*
Luigi Zoja - *Drugs, Addiction and Initiation*
Luigi Zoja & Donald Williams - *Jungian Reflections on September 11*
Jungian Congress Papers - *Jerusalem 1983: Symbolic & Clinical Approaches*
- *Berlin 1986: Archetype of Shadow in a Split World*
- *Paris 1989: Dynamics in Relationship*
- *Chicago 1992: The Transcendent Function*
- *Zürich 1995: Open Questions*
- *Florence 1998: Destruction and Creation*
- *Cambridge 2001*
- *Barcelona 2004: Edges of Experience*
- *Cape Town 2007: Journeys, Encounters*
- *Montreal 2010: Facing Multiplicity*
- *Copenhagen 2013: 100 Years on*
- *Kyoto 2016: Anima Mundi in Transition*
- *Vienna 2019: Encountering the Other*

Our books are available from your bookstore or from our distributors:

Baker & Taylor
30 Amberwood Parkway
Ashland OH 44805, USA
Phone: 419-281-5100
Fax: 419-281-0200
www.btpubservices.com

Gazelle Book Services Ltd.
White Cross Mills, High Town
Lancaster LAI 4XS, UK
Tel: +44 1524 528500
Email: sales@gazellebookservices.co.uk
www.gazellebookservices.co.uk

Daimon Verlag - Hauptstrasse 85 - CH-8840 Einsiedeln - Switzerland
Phone: (41)(55) 412 2266
Email: info@daimon.ch
Visit our website: **www.daimon.ch** or write for our complete catalog